# Teaching For Thinking

PSYCHOLOGY IN THE CLASSROOM: A SERIES ON APPLIED EDUCATIONAL PSYCHOLOGY

A collaborative project of APA Division 15 (Educational Psychology) and APA Books.

Barbara L. McCombs and Sharon McNeely, Series Editors

### Advisory Board

Sylvia Seidel, National Education Association

Debbie Walsh, Chicago Teachers Union, American Federation of Teachers

Ron Brandt, Executive Editor, Association for Supervision and Curriculum Development

Isadore Newton, University of Akron

Merlin Wittrock, University of California, Los Angeles

David Berliner, Arizona State University

Noreen Webb, University of California, Los Angeles

### Series Titles

*Becoming Reflective Students and Teachers With Portfolios and Authentic Assessment*—Paris & Ayres

*Creating Responsible Learners: The Role of a Positive Classroom Environment*—Ridley & Walthers

*Developing Self-Regulated Learners: Beyond Achievement to Self-Efficacy*—Zimmerman, Bonner, and Kovach

*Inventive Strategies for Teaching Mathematics*—Middleton & Goepfert

*Motivating Hard to Reach Students*—McCombs & Pope

*New Approaches to Literacy: Helping Students Develop Reading and Writing Skills*—Marzano & Paynter

*Overcoming Student Failure: Changing Motives and Incentives for Learning*—Covington & Teel

*Teaching for Thinking*—Sternberg & Spear-Swerling

### In Preparation

Designing Integrated Curricula—Jones, Rasmussen, & Lindberg

Effective Learning and Study Strategies—Weinstein & Hume

Positive Affective Climates—Mills & Timm

Dealing With Anxiety in the School—Tobias & Tobias

# Teaching For Thinking

Robert J. Sternberg and Louise Spear-Swerling

AMERICAN PSYCHOLOGICAL ASSOCIATION | WASHINGTON, DC

The work reported herein was supported under the Javits Act program (Grant #R206R00001 and Grant #R206R50001) as administered by the Office of Educational Research and Improvement, U.S. Department of Education. The findings and opinions expressed in this report do not reflect the positions or policies of the Office of Educational Research and Improvement or the U.S. Department of Education.

Published by
American Psychological Association
750 First Street, NE
Washington, DC 20002

Copies may be ordered from
APA Order Department
P.O. Box 2710
Hyattsville, MD 20784

In the UK and Europe, copies may be ordered from
American Psychological Association
3 Henrietta Street
Covent Garden, London
WC2E 8LU England

Typeset in Berkeley and Bell Gothic by University Graphics, Inc., York, PA
Printer: Data Reproductions Corporation, Rochester Hills, MI
Cover Designer: KINETIK Communication Graphics, Inc., Washington, DC
Technical/Production Editor: Edward B. Meidenbauer

**Library of Congress Cataloging-in-Publication Data**
Sternberg, Robert J.
    Teaching for thinking / Robert J. Sternberg and Louise Spear
-Swerling.
      p.  cm. — (Psychology in the classroom)
    Includes bibliographical references.
    ISBN 1-55798-375-5 (alk. paper)
    1. Thought and thinking — Study and teaching — United States.
2. Creative thinking — Study and teaching — United States.  I. Spear
-Swerling, Louise.  II. Title.  III. Series.
LB1590.3.S74   1996
370.15′2—dc20
                          96-20123
                            CIP

**British Library Cataloguing-in-Publication Data**
A CIP record is available from the British Library.

*Printed in the United States of America*
*First Edition*

This book is dedicated to our children, Seth and Sara Sternberg, and Olivia and David Swerling

# TABLE OF CONTENTS

# PREFACE

Over the past two decades, we've been thinking a lot about thinking. So when we were asked by Barbara McCombs and Sharon McNeely, editors of this series, to produce a book on *Teaching for Thinking*, we were delighted to have the opportunity to put down our thoughts in one place, and in an integrated fashion. Writing this book has been a valuable experience for us, and we hope that reading it will be a valuable experience for our readers as well. We have tried to put down in one place, in an organized fashion, much of what we have come to believe about how to teach effectively for thinking.

The organizing ideas for the entire volume come from Sternberg's triarchic (three-part) theory of thinking, according to which thinking is of three basic kinds: analytical, creative, and practical. Analytical thinking involves analyzing, judging, evaluating, comparing and contrasting, and examining. Creative thinking involves creating, discovering, producing, imagining, and supposing. Practical thinking involves practicing, using, applying, and implementing. Together, the three kinds of thinking are powerful tools for students, both in the classroom and outside it. The theory gives the book a unified perspective, but we have tried not to let ourselves be chained to the theory. When we had something to say that did not necessarily follow directly from the theory, we said it anyway!

Our book is for teachers of students in grades K through 12. Our mission is to help them understand the various kinds of thinking, and then to apply these understandings directly to their instruction. Thus, we have written a book that we believe is practical, but that is more than a "how-to" book: It is one that will give teachers ideas for teaching, but also a firm grasp of why we believe these ideas to be useful ones.

We hope our readers will gain as much pleasure from reading this book as we gained from writing it, because we truly believe that no goal of education is more important and, ultimately, pleasurable, than to teach students to think well.

A number of individuals have collaborated in the research described in this book. We wish to thank especially Janet Davidson, who collaborated with Sternberg in the work on insight. We also thank Sai Durvasula and Douglas Rau, who helped with preparation of the manuscript.

Robert J. Sternberg
Louise Spear-Swerling

# introduction

Jack points out to his pal, Tom, the boy Jack has identified as the stupidest in his class, Irvin. Jack, who considers himself the smartest in the class, likes to make fun of Irvin.

"You want to see what 'stupid' means, Tom? Watch this."

"Hey, Irvin. Here are two coins. Take whichever one you want. It's yours."

Irvin looks at the two coins, a nickel and a dime. He stares at them for a while, and then selects the larger coin, the nickel.

"Go ahead, Irv, take it, it's yours," laughs Jack.

Irvin takes the coin and walks away. An adult, who has been watching the transaction from a distance, walks up to Irvin and gently points out that the dime is worth more than the nickel, despite the dime's being smaller, and that Irvin has just cost himself five cents.

"Oh, I know that," replies Irvin, "but if I picked the dime, Jack never would ask me to choose between the two coins again, and this way, he'll keep asking me again and again. I've already collected over a dollar from him, and all I have to do is keep choosing the nickel."

## STATEMENT AND RATIONALE

This apocryphal story points out something we already intuitively know—that someone can be slow in school but think well outside it, and vice versa. The well-rehearsed question, "How can someone so smart be so dumb?", reminds us of how someone can be a good or a bad thinker, however well he or she may do in a school setting. Our book is about teaching students to be good thinkers, inside and outside of school settings.

The goal of this book is to help teachers promote effective student thinking. Students learn better when they think effectively about the material they are learning. Learning and thinking are not two distinct, independent entities. Rather, if students think to learn, they learn to think, and they learn what they need to know far more effectively than if they merely try to memorize. In the book, we show (a) what good thinking is, (b) a variety of strategies teachers can use to promote good thinking, and (c) how teachers can evaluate the thinking of their students. Any teacher who reads this book will be in a better position to promote high-quality thinking on the part of his or her students, and even to improve his or her own thinking as well. The mainstay of our approach is the triarchic theory of intelligence, which identifies three kinds of thinking: analytical, creative, and practical. Unfortunately, traditional schooling rewards only one kind of thinking—analytical. In the pages that follow, you will learn to identify, value, and nurture all three ways of thinking.

## OVERVIEW OF THIS BOOK

We divide the book into seven goals, each oriented toward a different aspect of promoting thinking. We begin each section by specifying a goal; then we show how to accomplish the goal; finally we provide some activities teachers can use to implement the goals.

The seven goals we have set out for our readers represent what we believe to be essential concepts, skills, and strategies that teachers will want to master in order to teach successfully for thinking. In Goal 1, we describe what we believe are three key ways of thinking, as well as the higher order mental processes underlying them. Goal 2 describes basic strategies that you can use to enhance the three ways of thinking. Goal 3 amplifies on these strategies by discussing the role of questioning in developing thinking skills. Goal 4 gets more specific, and describes targeted techniques for teaching the three ways of thinking. In Goal 5, we spotlight in particular, one of these ways of thinking, namely, creative and insightful thinking. In Goal 6, we discuss some general principles and pitfalls teachers encounter in implementing these (or any) strategies for teaching children to think. Finally, in Goal 7, we describe why even good thinkers can fail to be effective in school and in everyday life outside the school. We see that there is more to success in school and in life than higher order thinking. Thinking is an important part of the story, but by no means the whole story. A glossary of terms may be found at the end of the book, as well as a list of all the references we have cited.

## goal 1

### Understanding the Three Ways of Good Thinking and the Higher Order Thinking Processes Underlying Them

Two boys are walking in a forest. They are quite different. The first boy's teachers think he is smart, his parents think he is smart, and as a result, he thinks he is smart. He has good test scores, good grades, and other good paper credentials that will get him far in his scholastic life. Few people consider the second boy smart. His test scores are nothing great, his grades aren't so good, and his other paper credentials are, in general, marginal. At best, people would call him shrewd or street smart. As the two boys walk along in the forest, they encounter a problem: namely, a huge, furious, hungry-looking grizzly bear. It is charging straight at them. The first boy, calculating that the grizzly bear will overtake them in 17.3 seconds, panics. In this state, he looks at the second boy, who is calmly taking off his hiking boots and putting on his jogging shoes.

The first boy says to the second boy, "You must be crazy. There is no way we are going to outrun that grizzly bear!"

The second boy replies, "That's true. But all I have to do is outrun you!"

In the preceding story, both boys are smart, but they are smart in different ways. Let's discuss different ways of being smart and different ways of using the smarts one has. All tests measure only a small part of intelligence. Many people with modest test scores are nevertheless highly intelligent. To be intelligent is to think well in one or more of three different ways: analytical, creative, and practical (Sternberg, 1985a, 1988).

Table 1 shows how people can be smart in at least three major ways. One of the missing elements of our system of education is that typically only one of these ways is valued in tests and in the classroom. Yet no one way is any better than either of the others, and, ironically, the style of intelligence that schools most readily recognize as smart may well be less useful than the others to many students in their adult lives.

The table is based on Sternberg's (1985a, 1988, 1996) triarchic theory of human intelligence, according to which intelligence involves a balance of analytical, creative, and practical information processing. The theory has been val-

| Table 1 | Characteristics of Students Preferring Analytic, Creative, and Practical Thinking | | |
|---|---|---|---|
| **Analytic** | **Creative** | **Practical** | |
| High grades | Moderate to lower grades | Moderate to low grades | |
| High test scores | Moderate test scores | Moderate to low test scores | |
| Likes school | Feels confined by school | Feels bored by school | |
| Liked by teachers | Often viewed as a pain by teachers | Often viewed as disconnected by teachers | |
| "Fits" into school | Doesn't fit well into school | Doesn't fit well into school | |
| Follows directions | Doesn't like to follow directions | Likes to know what use task and directions serve | |
| Sees flaws in ideas | Likes to come up with own ideas | Likes to apply ideas in a pragmatic fashion | |
| Natural "critic" | Natural "ideas" person | Natural common sense | |
| Often prefers to be given directions | Likes to direct self | Likes to find self in practical settings | |

idated and implemented in a variety of settings (see, e.g., Sternberg, Wagner, Williams, & Horvath, 1995), and has been shown to be useful in educational settings (see, e.g., Sternberg, Ferrari, Clinkenbeard, & Grigorenko, in press). Most importantly, it is based on the view that there is more to intelligence than IQ, and that intelligence can be modified (Sternberg, 1986, 1987).

1. *Critical–analytic thinking.* Alice (a real student, but with her name changed) was the teacher's dream. She scored high on tests, performed well in class, and, in general, did everything that a teacher would expect a bright student to do. The result was that Alice was always considered to be at or near the top of her class. Her high test scores were accepted as a valid indicant of her ability to do outstanding work throughout her academic career. Yet by the time Alice was finished with graduate school in psychology, she was performing at a very modest level. About 70 to 80 percent of her classmates were doing better. Alice-types occur at all levels of schooling.

For example, last semester one of our students tested a first-grader we will call Billy. Billy was only 5 years old—he had started school early. In October of first grade, he tested at a third-grade level in oral reading and could decode almost any word. His reading comprehension also was excellent. When asked to write something, he produced a coherent story a page long that included commas and quotation marks. He also requested permission to look up the spelling of some of the more difficult words in a dictionary—which he accomplished on his own when permission was granted! According to all accounts, this boy was not in any kind of instructional program in preschool; he was simply fascinated by books and words, and he spent a lot of time on his own trying to figure out how to read and spell. Here's a child almost everybody recognizes as smart.

The question that naturally arises is, what went wrong with Alice, and might with Billy? The answer, quite simply, is that although Alice was excellent at remembering and analyzing other people's ideas, she was not very good at coming up with ideas of her own. Consequently, she faltered in advanced schooling, where (as in life) it is necessary to come up with ideas of one's own. Similarly, although Billy's academic skills certainly are impressive, he will require more than just a high level of academic achievement in order to do well in advanced schooling and in adult life.

If we think about schooling as preparation for the world of work, we need to be concerned about whether schooling requires and develops creative thinking, because for Alice, and eventually for Billy, to stay competitive in most jobs, it is and will be necessary for them to come up with their own ideas.

In science, for example, one needs more than the ability to memorize facts in a book or to solve ready-made problems at the ends of chapters. The practice of science requires the ability to come up with creative, significant ideas that make a difference to the field and, ultimately, to the world. People who generate important scientific ideas are not necessarily those who are best at memorizing facts or solving textbook problems. Indeed, they may be people who do not particularly like to do these things and who therefore do not show themselves at their best in school settings.

The same dynamic applies in other occupations. Consider writing or art. It is one thing to succeed in writing good essays when told what to write about, or to draw nice pictures when told what the pictures should show. It is quite another thing to come up with one's own ideas for stories or pictures. For example, outside a classroom, one of us once observed roughly two dozen pictures of children's houses. They were nice pictures of houses, but it was clear that the teacher had told the students what to draw—it did not seem likely that 24 children had independently decided to draw pictures of houses. In the real world of art and writing, though, someone is not always there to tell the artist or writer what their composition should deal with. Indeed, creative writers and artists are, almost by definition, people who come up with their own imaginative ideas.

The problem with the current situation is, of course, that telling students what to do is often unrealistic with respect to what the students will be required to do later. Educators need to stop always formulating problems for students and instead sometimes urge the students to formulate problems for themselves.

One could argue that most students will not become scientists or writers or artists, but the situation is no different in a very pragmatic occupation like business. Many of the executives interviewed during our studies of practical intelligence complain that one can hire a top-level graduate of a business school and get someone who may be good at analyzing textbook cases, but who is unable to come up with innovative ideas for new business products or services, rearrangements that create more shelf space, or ways to stay competitive with similar industries in other countries.

The point, of course, is that there are large gaps between the kind of performance needed for success in a business setting and the kind of performance needed for success in schools, even schools that are supposed to be quite practical in training students for the world of business. Thus, we often end up with adults who are unable to do what is expected of them.

This same problem even afflicts the study of education

itself. It is one thing to get A's in education courses and quite another to succeed when called upon to be innovative in a classroom setting. We know from experience just how challenging classroom situations can be. For example, several years ago one of us was giving a lecture at the University of Puerto Rico, and found himself confronting a serious classroom management problem, namely, the professors of education in the audience just were not listening. For whatever reasons, they had decided to tune out, and they were walking around, in and out of the room, speaking among themselves, and generally not being very attentive.

He tried the standard, uncreative techniques one learns in the course of training to be a teacher. He tried lowering his voice in the hope that these professors would then lower their voices so that they would be able to hear him. Of course, he was assuming that they wanted to hear, an assumption that proved false. Instead, they appeared to be grateful that he had lowered his voice so that they could hear themselves better. He then tried asking them to be quiet, but that didn't work, either. Finally, after he had given up, a woman in the audience shot up and said something in rapid-fire Spanish. After that, you could have heard a pin drop, and the audience remained silent and attentive for the rest of the session.

What did she say? She had capitalized on her understanding that Puerto Rico is a shame culture, not a guilt culture. The author's attempts to make the audience feel guilty might have worked in the mainland United States, but were ineffective in Puerto Rico. In contrast, the woman pointed out to the audience that, if they continued to be noisy, the author would leave with a poor impression of the University of Puerto Rico. He would then report this bad impression to others. She said that the audience had no right to convey a bad impression and thereby to cast shame on the university. This appeal was effective in achieving the behavioral change that he had unsuccessfully sought.

Why is it that the students whom we consider to be bright tend to be bright like Alice? In other words, why are they so often test-smart, but not necessarily smart in other ways?

We think that children are not born to be smart only in this limited way, but that we shape them to be. Our system of education, in essence, creates Alices by continually reinforcing or rewarding students for being test-smart. Indeed, the main lesson that students learn is that it pays to be smart like Alice. As rewards, you receive good grades, good placements in high tracks, awards, and later, impressive college admissions.

One indication that schools mold students into Alices comes from Joe Glick's study of the Kpelle tribe (Cole, Gay, Glick, & Sharp, 1971). Glick asked adult members of the tribe to sort terms into categories. For example, they might be asked to sort names of fruits (apple, orange, grapefruit) or names of vegetables (celery, lettuce, broccoli) or names of vehicles (bus, boat, car). Glick found that the Kpelle sorted functionally. For example, they would sort "apple" with "eat" and "car" with "gas" because people eat apples and cars use gas.

In our culture, only young children sort functionally. The Kpelle's functional kind of sorting behavior is considered stupid when it is done by an adult. Older children and adults are expected to sort taxonomically (putting fruits together) or hierarchically (putting the word "fruit" over the names of different fruits and then perhaps putting the word "food" over the whole lot).

Glick tried, without actually instructing them on how to sort taxonomically, to get the Kpelle to sort in other ways. When he was about to conclude that they simply did not have the mental ability to do things any differently, he decided as a last resort to ask them how a stupid person would do the task. At this point, they sorted taxonomically, and with no trouble at all. Why would the Kpelle consider taxonomic sorting stupid? The answer is that the Kpelle did not grow up in our educational system and— even more important—did not take our tests. In everyday life, humans tend to think functionally. We think of eating apples or using gas in cars. We learn to think taxonomically in school, but for the most part this kind of thinking remains limited to artificial settings. A problem arises, therefore, when advanced students or career aspirants have to start thinking in ways that they have not been conditioned in school to think, that is, when they need to start turning out their own ideas rather than reciting back or analyzing ideas that other people have had.

Because these kinds of skills have not been actively encouraged or selected for, students tend not to develop them. In this respect, then, our schools essentially mislead and misprepare students by developing and rewarding a set of skills that will be important in later life, but much less important than they are in school.

2. *Creative–synthetic thinking.* A student whom we shall call Barbara exhibits a second way of being intelligent. Barbara's grades were good, although by no means spectacular. Her undergraduate teachers thought that she was just terrific, despite the fact that her test scores were very weak.

When Barbara applied to our graduate program in psychology, she was rejected by an almost unanimous vote. In fact, one of the authors was the only person who voted to admit her. Even though Barbara had included a portfolio of her work that demonstrated a high degree of competence, the other admissions people made their decisions largely on the basis of her test scores. In other words, they had more confidence in fallible and often weak predictors of creative work than they had in the work itself. We often see this odd situation in education today. The predictor of the performance has become more important than the performance itself! Barbaras do not occur just at the graduate level.

Consider Olivia as another good example of creative abilities. At age six, Olivia had been a good solid student—above average in most areas, but not the kind of exceptional early reader and writer that Billy was. What teachers repeatedly commented on was that Olivia was "very creative," "an independent thinker," that she "has an unusual way of thinking," and so forth. Some of her art work was even selected to represent her school at a regional art show.

Olivia's creative ability was not limited to art. For instance, Olivia's favorite subject in school was science, and she frequently initiated her own science projects at home, such as growing bacteria, gathering insect specimens outdoors, and so on. Once she used an old deflated balloon and a diagram of the human digestive tract from a book to make her own "model" of a stomach and intestines. She once saw a children's game on television that interested her; instead of pestering her parents to buy it for her (which she knew would be futile), she constructed her own cardboard version of it. Thus, she was really good at generating interesting ideas and at carrying them out independently.

Fortunately, many of Olivia's teachers truly appreciated her creative abilities. But it was apparent that not everyone valued her abilities as highly as they valued abilities like Billy's. Some people even viewed her negatively, because she tended to have strong preferences for the kinds of problems she wanted to work on and for how she wanted to do things.

Why has Barbara's future been jeopardized, and why is Olivia's at risk as well? Why do teachers, professors, school administrators, and corporate executives pay more attention to predictors than to performance? And in general, why do they pay so much attention to results on tests of IQ and related abilities?

## OVERUSE OF TEST SCORES

We believe that, to achieve a more balanced perspective on testing, we need to understand why teachers rely upon test scores so heavily. In our opinion there are at least five reasons why test scores tend to be overused. These reasons not only result in creative thinking of students being undervalued. They are themselves a block to creative development on the part of teachers and of schools. Basically, they result in an entrenched status quo that blocks creativity at all levels of the educational process.

The first is the *quantitative pseudoprecision reason*. By that we mean that people overuse quantitative data because these data appear to be so precise. People see numbers and assume that they have a lot to tell us. In fact, we know from research that people will use numbers in making decisions even if they are told that the numbers are irrelevant to the decision that they have to make. It seems likely, then, that if people believe that test scores are at least somewhat relevant, they will give these figures great weight in making decisions. The problem is that the numbers are actually of only very limited validity, no matter how exact they seem to be. People need to recognize that tests are quite limited in what their results can predict, notwithstanding appearances to the contrary.

A second reason that people overuse quantitative data is what we call the *culpability reason*, a fear of being blamed for not having used available numbers. Why should a person be criticized for not using numbers?

Suppose that a person making an admission decision goes with the numbers, and the person predicted to succeed does not subsequently succeed. Who is to blame? In practice, people tend to blame the testing company, the school from which the student came, or practically anybody except the person who made the admissions decision. That person cannot be blamed, having decided on the basis of paper credentials. Thus, he or she made a safe decision.

Suppose, on the other hand, that this person had admitted someone like Barbara, someone with doubtful paper credentials. What happens if that student flounders? Then the admitting official is in a position of potential culpability. Critics can go back, look at the test scores, and conclude that the person who should be blamed for the mistake is the person who made the decision to admit a poor prospect. After all, anyone could have looked at the paper credentials and seen that the student would not succeed!

So to admit a student with marginal scores is to put oneself on the line. If that student does not succeed—and in any category of students, there will be some who do not—the reviewing official's reputation is jeopardized. People may even wonder why a person who cannot make such a simple selection or placement decision is doing that job.

The third reason is the *similarity reason*. Obviously, the people making the admissions decisions must, at some time, have gained admission themselves. In other words, their test scores were high enough to get them into whatever kind of program about which they are now making decisions. We tend to view people who are like ourselves as smart. Because the people now making admissions decisions once had decent scores themselves, it is natural for them to favor applicants with pretty high scores. Thus the system perpetuates itself as people continually choose others like themselves, and the result is that we keep getting more Alices and fewer Barbaras.

We call the fourth reason the *publication reason*. Because test scores are published, a lot has come to hinge on them. For example, in our home state of Connecticut, the statewide mastery test scores appear to be a major determinant of property values. How has this happened? Simple. The local newspapers report test scores district by district. When people read the newspapers, they take test scores as proxies for the quality of schooling in a particular locale. They become reluctant to pay high prices for real estate in areas with lower test scores; and conversely, because they want the best for their children, they will pay more for real estate in areas that have schools with higher test scores.

With private schools, colleges, and universities, the situation is very similar. The reputation of institutions of higher education hinges in part on the perceived quality of the institution's students, and the perceived quality is higher if the test scores are higher. Again, the result is a self-perpetuating system that creates a strong incentive to keep scores high, even though these scores provide very narrow measures of the institution's quality.

Our fifth and final reason for people's overreliance on quantified data is one we refer to as the *rain-dance reason*. Here's the idea. Suppose that the authors were invited to lecture at a town in another state. So we go to the place, find it attractive, and would like to tour around. Typically, though, we find that we do not have the time—we must go in and out almost immediately. A year later, we decide that we want to return, and the question is, how can we get ourselves invited back? We know that our former hosts won't reinvite us to hear our talks on thinking because we've already given those.

Now suppose further that the place is a nice town in the Southwest of the United States, or perhaps in Israel, or any place with a really dry climate. We just tell the people there that, for a specified fee, we can make it rain, and that if we don't, we will give them double their money back. How can they turn us down? They invite us to visit and make it rain. We go and the next morning we do a rain dance. After we do the rain dance, we spend the rest of the day touring. Of course, it may not rain after we do the dance. Probably it won't. In fact, probably everyone doubts that our doing a rain dance will produce rain. That night, our hosts will ask for double their money back.

So we say that they must be kidding—in a severe drought zone, they can't expect a single rain dance to make it rain. Sometimes two, three, four, or more applications of the rain dance are needed before it rains. Accordingly, we continue to do the rain dance each morning and tour the rest of the day. Eventually, of course, it rains. We thank the local residents for their hospitality (and our fee) and go home.

The point of this story is that superstitions persist by virtue of the great difficulty encountered in refuting them. Indeed, superstitions are, by their nature, almost undebunkable. People have believed in rain dances for thousands of years precisely because, if someone dances long enough, eventually it will rain.

None of us, of course, thinks that we have superstitions. We have *beliefs*. Nonetheless, it is easy to see that we are all subject to superstitions. One only has to observe people waiting for an elevator. Even after the call button has been pressed, people will continue to press the button. The expectation is that the more one presses the button, the sooner the elevator will come—a belief, of course, that is false.

There is a similar sort of superstition at work in education. Administrators and teachers (as well as the students themselves) often believe that people with test scores below a certain point cannot successfully do the work in a given program or institution. Because of this belief, administrators do not give them the chance to do the work. As a result, everyone can go on believing year after year that people with scores below that point cannot do the work because no one has ever encountered people with lower scores who are doing the work. Generations of teachers and administrators have set up a system that precludes evidence that might contradict this belief.

We know from experience that this rain-dance problem is not merely hypothetical. As a student in elementary school, one of us was beset by test anxiety and thus did very poorly on intelligence tests. The psychologist would come into the room to administer the test, and the author would panic, with the predictable result. Consequently, during the first 3 years of elementary school, his teachers did not believe that he was capable of producing very good work. As someone who is eager to please, he gave them exactly what they expected: mediocre work. The teachers were happy that his work was what they expected, and he was happy, more or less, that they were happy.

In fourth grade, he happened to have a teacher who believed that he was capable of doing better. He wanted to please this teacher, too, so he did better. But the irony is that he could have continued going through school doing mediocre work had it not been for that one teacher who believed in him.

We have heard other people tell similar stories that reveal an error people make over and over again. People create their own self-fulfilling prophecies (it will rain if we dance; students with low test scores are not capable of certain work), and then, when the prophecies come true, they conclude that their reasoning must have been correct. Often, however, nothing could be further from the truth.

For instance, one of us hired Barbara as a research associate because he believed that she showed much better potential than the test scores indicated. And he was not disappointed. Her work as a research associate was highly creative and innovative. Two years later, she was admitted as the top pick into our program. But do you suppose that Barbara's case changed the system? If anything, people's reaction was to regard Barbara as an odd exception to a sound rule. We need to open up our thinking and reappraise our educational superstitions if we are ever to change the way our educational system functions. Although, after many years of effort, things are loosening up, we still have far to go.

3. *Practical–contextual thinking* When Celia (not her real name) applied to our graduate program in psychology, she had grades that were good but not great, test scores that were good but not great, and letters of recommendation that were good but not great. In fact, just about everything in her application seemed to be good but not great. Naturally, we admitted Celia because every program needs people who are good but not great. Indeed, in our program, her work proved to be exactly what we had predicted: good, but not great—so we figured we hit it on that one.

But what a surprise Celia gave us when it came to getting a job: Everyone wanted to hire Celia! That raised an intriguing question. Why would someone who lacked Alice's analytic ability and Barbara's creative ability do so spectacularly well in the job market?

The answer is actually very simple. Celia was something like the second boy in the opening bear-in-the-forest story. She had an abundance of practical intelligence, or simple common sense. She could go into an environment, figure out what she needed to do to thrive there, and then do it.

For example, Celia knew how to interview effectively, how to interact well with other students, and how to get her work done. She also was aware of what kinds of things do and do not work. In other words, she was street smart in an academic setting. She knew something that is true, though seldom acknowledged: that in school, as well as life, one needs a certain amount of practical smartness in order to adapt to the environment. These talents can be seen in younger children as well.

For instance, one of us heard a television news story involving a child whose mother was epileptic. The child was about five or six years old. The mother had had a seizure just as she was about to get into the shower, and she was lying unconscious in the tub with scalding water pouring over her. There was no one else in the house but the little boy, who called 911, gave the dispatcher directions to his house, and so on. But the thing that really impressed us is that, before calling 911, the boy turned on the cold-water tap full force to keep his mother from being even more badly burned. He had also tried to turn off the hot-water tap, but it was too hot for him to turn it off.

Another example involves a child from our own experience, whom we will call Debbie. Debbie was a student of one of us years ago when the author was a learning-disabilities resource teacher. Debbie was 10 years old, in the fifth grade, and she, along with a group of three other fifth-graders, came to the author for help in basic academic subjects. Debbie's IQ was somewhere in the 70s, a good 20 to 30 points below the IQs of the three other children in her group. In fact, Debbie had once been placed in a class for retarded children. (This was in the early to middle 1970s, when children with "borderline" IQs ended up in mental retardation placements much more often than they do today.) Indeed, Debbie did seem to have a significantly harder time than did the other children in her group in acquiring academic skills and with analytical types of tasks (e.g., with higher level reading comprehension questions or problem solving in math).

However, when the four children were "mainstreamed" into a regular classroom full-time, surprisingly, it was Debbie who was most successful. Debbie definitely had "practical intelligence"—she knew how to approach the teacher to ask for help, how to function independently in a regular-classroom setting, how to get along with other children, and so on. Debbie was one of those few children who actually *solicit* constructive criticism about how she can "make it" in a regular classroom. And she wasn't just sitting there being compliant but not learning anything. Rather, she made the best possible use of the abilities she had, whereas the other children in her group, despite their higher IQs, often failed to mobilize their abilities effectively without the constant adult direction and supervision available in a special-education setting.

Whereas almost everyone would accept Alice and Billy as smart, and many people would regard Barbara and Olivia as smart (albeit in their own ways), few people would think of Celia and certainly not of Debbie as smart. They might concede that Celia and Debbie have common sense, but would not see that as part of intelligence. They might even say that Celia and Debbie are manipulative and reject the idea that being manipulative is an element of intelligence.

Not so. The kind of practical intelligence that Celia and Debbie exhibited is every bit as important as Alice's analytic or Barbara's synthetic intelligence. The reason is that different situations call for different kinds of intelligence. Furthermore, if teachers value only one kind of intelligence in school, we will seriously underestimate a lot of students. We will peg them as much less intelligent than they really are.

This tendency to undervalue certain forms of intelligence became apparent in our own research in California. We compared conceptions of intelligence among parents from different ethnic groups (Okagaki & Sternberg, 1993). We found that the more parents emphasize in their conception of intelligence social competence skills, such as getting along with peers and helping out the family, the less bright their own children look according to the standards of the schools. In other words, the mismatch between what the parents emphasized in their environment and what the schools required in their environment resulted in kids who might be quite competent in the home and community setting, but who would be judged as intellectually lacking in school.

Along a similar line of inquiry, Shirley Heath (1983) compared the language behavior of children in three communities:

□ Trackton, a lower social class Black community

□ Roadville, a lower social class White community

□ Gateway, a middle social class White community.

Heath found that the children from Trackton performed quite a bit worse than the children from Roadville or Gateway as soon as the children started school, but that the idea of how smart children are in school may be largely dependent on the match between parental and school conceptions of intelligence. The children in Trackton, therefore, might actually have been no less intelligent than the children in Roadville or Gateway.

For example, parents in Trackton were found to emphasize the importance of nonverbal communication. To communicate successfully in Trackton, it was necessary to be very adept at nonverbal cues, both with respect to understanding them and with respect to transmitting them. In Roadville and Gateway, on the other hand, more emphasis was placed on verbal skills, an emphasis that was a better match to the demands of the school. As a result, children from Roadville and Gateway appeared smarter than did children from Trackton, but they may actually have been no smarter. Once again, the middle class (especially the White middle class) benefited from the match between school values and home and community values.

It is quite plausible to argue that White middle-class culture undervalues the importance of nonverbal communication. For example, many boring teachers or professors can go on being boring year after year, precisely because they ignore the nonverbal communication of the audience. None of the students have the courage to risk an F by *telling* the teachers or professors that they are boring. Furthermore, this behavior certainly would not be practically intelligent! If the educators were to pay attention to nonverbal cues, they might well realize their failure to command attention and might even do something about it.

Sensitivity to nonverbal communication can be a key to success in an interview setting also. Information as to how well an interview is going is almost exclusively nonverbal. Interviewers know that they are not supposed to reveal their feelings about the person being interviewed. At times, there might be nothing they would rather say than, "Please leave now. I know that we have another 25 minutes left in the interview, but we both know that you are wasting my time and I am wasting yours." The interviewer may feel that way, but certainly cannot say so. Nevertheless, the interviewer's feelings are likely to leak out nonverbally. If the applicant is sensitive to the nonverbal communication, he or she at least has a chance of changing the way the interview is going.

In short, the ways of Trackton have something to teach us all. A child from Roadville or Gateway would look as stupid in Trackton as a child from Trackton would look in

Roadville or Gateway. We need to acknowledge the multiple styles of intelligence.

It is interesting as well to compare Roadville with Gateway. When the children from these two communities start school, they look roughly comparable. Within a few years, however, the White middle-class children from Gateway are doing better than the White lower-class children from Roadville. What happened? Do the Roadville children have some kind of "inherited cumulative deficit," as some would have us believe? We believe that the explanation is a lot simpler: that the views about the nature of education and intelligence that are commonly held in Roadville render the children there less smart *appearing* in school.

For example, parents in Roadville are more likely to believe that their role as teachers stops when the children start school; at that point, parents stop intervening in their children's education. They, like many parents of low socioeconomic status, have limited educations themselves, and may feel intimidated by the school, or ill-equipped to help, especially as their children get older (e.g., Snow, Barnes, Chandler, Goodman, & Hemphill, 1991). Gateway parents, on the other hand, continue to intervene, to the advantage of their children.

Moreover, parents from Roadville emphasize memory in their concept of intelligence, whereas parents from Gateway emphasize reasoning. As the years go by and reasoning becomes more important, the children from Gateway become progressively more advantaged.

Even in adulthood, there is evidence that many people possess contextual intelligence that is quite different from IQ-like intelligence. For example, our work on the practical intelligence of managers shows no significant degree of statistical association between practical and academic intelligence (Sternberg, Wagner, & Okagaki, 1993). Steve Ceci's work on bettors at a race track found results that were consistent with ours (Ceci & Liker, 1986). Ceci determined that the average IQ in a group of successful bettors was approximately 97, or slightly below average. Along the same lines, Lave, Murtaugh, and de la Roche (1984) showed that women shoppers who could easily compute mentally the better value between two products were hardly able to do the same operations if they were presented in paper-and-pencil format.

In sum, context matters. One cannot consider intelligence in isolation from context. To do so may lead to seriously erroneous conclusions about children's capacity to learn. All the investigations described above suggest that practical intelligence matters, but unfortunately it is not what tests measure, nor is it sufficiently emphasized in schools. Educators need to begin to consider not only the intelligence of Alice, but also that of Barbara and Celia.

Of course, although people usually have a preferred style of intelligence, they do not use only one style exclusively. In everyone, there is some combination of analytic, creative, and practical intelligence. We need to foster *all* these aspects of intelligence, not to favor just one. In addition, we need to recognize that people who are really smart are people who figure out (a) what it is they are good at, (b) what it is they are not good at, and (c) what they can do to make the most of their strengths, while remediating or compensating for their weaknesses.

In other words, the most functionally intelligent people are not necessarily the ones with the greatest degree of intelligence in any of its three styles. Being smart in everyday life means making the most of what one has, not conforming to any preset stereotypical pattern of what others may consider smart. It is this view of intelligence and of styles of intelligence that we need to adopt in order to obtain the most from our students and ourselves. Being academically smart, like Alice and Billy, is important in school and even, to an extent, in later life; but there is more to intelligence than what tests measure!

## HIGHER ORDER THINKING PROCESSES

In the triarchic theory, the same basic set of thinking skills underlies all three ways of thinking. Analytic people are particularly adept in applying these skills to familiar and often academic kinds of problems. Creative people are particularly adept at applying them to relatively novel problems. Practical people are particularly adept at applying them to everyday problems.

After decades of bickering, many research psychologists seem to be reaching at least a partial consensus as to what the higher order processes are. Our version of this view (Sternberg, 1977, 1979, 1980a, 1980b, 1981b, 1985a), which is similar in some ways to those of Butterfield and Belmont (1977), Campione and Brown (1979), Carroll (1981), Hunt (1978), Pellegrino and Glaser (1980), and Snow (1979), is that good thinking consists of a set of developed thinking and learning skills used in academic and everyday problem solving.

## COGNITIVE SKILLS

Although the following list of seven such skills is neither exhaustive nor mutually exclusive, we believe it reasonably represents the skills needed for adaptive task performance in a great variety of situations (Sternberg, 1981b; see Baron & Sternberg, 1987, for other views). Table 2 shows how these skills apply in school subject matter areas.

1. *Problem identification.* Here, you need both to recognize that you have a problem and to define what the problem is. Consider, for example, a student assigned to write a social studies paper on a topic of his or her choice. The quality of the outcome in large part depends on the choice of topic; some topics will not yield an interesting paper regardless of what one does with them. Although no topic guarantees a good paper, some seem to preclude a good one.

The ability to identify problems is measured indirectly by ability tests. Distracters on intelligence and other tests are frequently the right answers to the wrong problems. On arithmetic problem-solving tests, distracters are often correct answers to sub-problems of the full problem, and thus might be correct outcomes for intermediate stages of problem solution. Returning to Alice (the critical–analytical thinker mentioned earlier), note that she is someone

| | Subject | |
|---|---|---|
| Components | Mathematics | English |

**Table 2** — Cognitive Processes Underlying the Three Kinds of Thinking: Applications for Mathematics, English, Science, and Social Studies

Problem identification:

| Components | Mathematics | English |
|---|---|---|
| 1. Recognizing and defining the existence of a problem | Are there different infinities?<br><br>How might we characterize a straight line algebraically? | Why was Upton Sinclair dissatisfied with many aspects of society?<br><br>How did Sinclair Lewis poke fun at middle-class America in *Babbitt*? |
| 2. Process selection | What steps do you take to borrow when doing subtraction? | What steps do you take in writing a book review? |
| 3. Representation of information | How can 3/5 and .6 both refer to the same quantity? | How can you diagram a particular sentence so that the diagram and the sentence "say" the same thing? |
| 4. Strategy formulation | Show a proof that all congruent triangles are also similar. | What are the possible orders for the steps in writing a book review? |
| 5. Allocation of resources | How long should it take you to do your math homework? | Is it worth spending the time to learn English grammar? Why or why not? |
| 6. Solution monitoring | How can you tell when your efforts to solve an arithmetic word problem are not getting you anywhere? | Is your essay turning out as you had hoped or are you losing sight of what you thought you were going to accomplish? |
| 7. Evaluating solutions | Does your solution to a particular problem make sense? | Have you proofread your essay? |

| | Subject | |
|---|---|---|
| Components | Science | Social Studies |

Problem identification:

| | | |
|---|---|---|
| 1. Recognizing and defining the existence of a problem | Light seems to be neither a wave nor a particle, so what is it? | The stock market is undergoing unacceptably large fluctuations lately, so what can be done? |
| | Will a vaccine for AIDS be difficult to formulate because the AIDS virus mutates so rapidly? | Is the U.S. having difficulty reducing its national deficit because of increased defense spending coupled with a decrease in taxes? |
| 2. Process selection | What steps would constitute an experimental test of whether aspirin helps prevent heart attacks? | What steps do we need to take to convince other countries that the U.S. is genuinely interested in peace? |
| 3. Representation of information | What is the chemical formula for sulfuric acid? | How can we represent the topography of various land masses on a map? |
| 4. Strategy formulation | In what order should the steps of the experiment be executed? | In what order should the steps be taken to convince other countries of our sincerity? |
| 5. Allocation of resources | How much should be spent on basic versus applied research on superconductors? | How much of the national budget should be devoted to welfare? |
| 6. Solution monitoring | Are we making adequate progress in developing treatments for cancer? | Is U.S. policy toward dictatorships actually succeeding in isolating them? |
| 7. Evaluating solutions | Is generic aspirin as effective as brand-name aspirin? | Did the Civil Rights Act actually guarantee everyone civil rights? |

who may be quite adept at solving problems, but who is not necessarily adept at identifying good problems to solve.

2. *Process selection.* In order to solve a problem successfully, one must select or discover a set of appropriate processes. Consider the steps in writing a research paper on, say, the declining role of the United States as "the world's policeman." One needs to identify possible relevant sources of information, discarding sources that are irrelevant; seek those sources in libraries or elsewhere; cull from those sources information that is relevant, and ignore information that is irrelevant; evaluate the credibility of the various sources; and so on.

Intelligence tests measure process selection ability, but again, only indirectly. In order to solve a test problem, an individual must select processes that will yield a correct answer. Except for rare cases, the tests do not separate the ability to select a set of processes from the ability to execute them. One of these rare exceptions is the kind of arithmetic problem-solving test that asks examinees what operations (addition, subtraction, multiplication, division) they would use to solve problems, but does not require them to execute the operations. A potential problem with this kind of test is that individuals are not always aware of their own process-selection practices; forcing them to bring these practices out into the open may change the nature of the problem solving required by the test. Process selection is itself a higher order process, and is, like problem identification, an important prerequisite for successful problem solving.

3. *Representation of information.* In most tasks requiring intelligent performance, the individual must represent information in a useful way, both internally (in one's head) and externally (on paper). A student collecting information for the paper on the U.S. as the world's policeman might organize his or her notes by authors of books and articles, or by topics. The latter organization is usually more effective, although probably less widely used. Similarly, encoding the information by topic will be much more useful in later recall than encoding the information by author.

Again, this particular skill is measured by ability tests, but only indirectly. Information that is more effectively represented internally (in long-term memory) is more easily retrieved in verbal tests than is information that is ineffectively represented. Likewise, the effective external representation of new information, such as by a diagram in the solution of an arithmetic problem, can often expedite problem solving in a way that use of symbols without an accompanying diagram may not.

4. *Strategy formation.* Selection of processes and a representation for information must be accompanied by the formulation of a strategy for sequencing processes in the order they act on the representation. Ineffective sequencing of steps can result not only in wasted time and effort, but in a poor product. For example, students often try to write introductions to papers before their research is completed, figuring that although the research may affect the main body of the paper, it should have little or no effect on a section that merely describes the goals and motivations behind the paper. But as experienced authors know, goals and motivations often change as a project progresses, and sometimes the resultant paper isn't anything like the paper one originally intended to write.

Strategy formulation is measured by ability tests, but again usually indirectly. Some tests, such as the mathematics portion of the *Scholastic Assessment Test*, have certain items that are particularly sensitive to individual differences in strategy selection. These items normally can be solved by applying a pedestrian strategy, but executing these items in this way is particularly time-consuming and ineffective. The items can also be solved quickly through insightful application of a novel strategy, but in order to arrive at that strategy, examinees have to be willing to invest time in strategy selection, rather than blindly executing the first (usually pedestrian) strategy that comes to mind.

5. *Allocation of resources.* Virtually all tasks can be allocated only limited amounts of time and other resources. An important decision to make in performing a task is how to

allocate time to the various components in order to optimize performance. Poor time allocation may turn a potentially excellent product into a mediocre one. Students commonly allow insufficient time for actually writing a paper. They spend a great deal of time doing research, but then find they do not have enough time to write the kind of paper they could, on the basis of their research, if they had more time. As a result, the final product does not well represent the work that went into it.

Intelligence tests indirectly measure allocation of processing resources by, in most cases, allowing a limited amount of time for solving many items. Examinees who tend to spend too much time on a few items, or who rush through lots of items, are at a disadvantage compared with students who use their time flexibly, spending on a given item the amount of time it deserves—no more or less.

6. *Solution monitoring.* As individuals proceed through a task, they must keep track of what they have already done, what they are currently doing, and what remains to be done. They must also check that their skills have been applied to the task in a way that is bringing them closer to solution. In writing a research paper, it is important to keep track of sources that were already consulted, so as not to waste time reconsulting them. One further needs to keep track of what kinds of information have been collected and what kinds still need to be collected.

Ability tests indirectly measure individuals' abilities to monitor their solution processes; success in monitoring such processes should be related to success in solving a wide variety of problems.

7. *Evaluating solutions.* This step involves sensitivity to feedback and translating the feedback into an action plan. In performing a task, there are often various sources of internal and external feedback. Internal feedback derives from one's own perceptions of how well a task is being performed, and external feedback comes from other people's perceptions. Sensitivity to feedback is a major determinant of a person's potential to improve his or her work. This

ability is probably at least as relevant for future as for present task performance.

Sensitivity to feedback is probably measured only minimally, if at all, by current ability tests. But tests of the kind proposed by Vygotsky (1978) and Feuerstein (1979), which provide graded feedback in order to assess learning potential (or what Vygotsky referred to as a "zone of potential development"), seem well able to measure this ability. Understanding feedback is one thing; knowing what to do with it is another. People are sometimes aware of what they do incorrectly but don't know how to use feedback to change their performance. Yet sensitivity to feedback without the ability to translate it into an action plan is worthless. In some cases, such as recognizing the limited usefulness of encyclopedias, the nature of the action plan may be obvious. In other cases—such as knowing that one tends to skip around from one topic to another in one's writing without fully developing any of the topics—the formation of an action plan may be more difficult. Again, ability tests seem to provide only the most limited measurement of this skill, to the extent that they measure it at all.

## SUMMARY

In discussing Goal 1, we have described three kinds of thinking and the higher order thinking processes underlying them. We have discussed, in particular, the importance of analytical, creative, and practical thinking in education. We have also discussed some educational practices that thwart the recognition and development of the three kinds of thinking. Next we discuss some teaching strategies to enhance thinking.

## GOAL 1: SELF-DIRECTED QUESTIONS AND ACTIVITIES

**1** Describe an "Alice," "Barbara," and "Celia" from your own experience and how each exemplifies analytic, creative, and practical thinking abilities. How have each of these individuals fared in school and (if they are adults) in adult life? Were their experiences consistent with the kinds of problems discussed in the text? If so, in which ways?

**2** Discuss some reasons why test scores tend to be disproportionately influential in educational decision making

**3** If you were in a position to decide what kinds of tests would be used in your district, would you employ standardized tests or would you discard them entirely? Why? What other sources of information about students' abilities (besides standardized tests) might you use?

**4** Are there practices in your own school district, school, or classroom that tend to encourage students to develop only analytic ways of thinking and not creative or practical abilities? If so, what are these practices? If not, what are the practices that encourage creative and practical thinking?

**5** Describe some of the higher order processes that underlie the different ways of thinking. To what extent are these processes measured by typical standardized tests?

**6** If you could dramatically improve your own performance in one of these higher order processes, which one would you pick up and why?

1   Alice is an individual who exemplifies high analytic abilities and who tends to perform very well on typical academic tasks such as standardized tests. Barbara exemplifies strong creative abilities and excels at coming up with good ideas. Celia exemplifies good common sense and high practical intelligence. Of course, individual experiences may vary; however, although Alices tend to do better in school than do Barbaras or Celias, each of the latter may well outperform an Alice in adult life outside of school.

2   These reasons include the quantitative pseudoprecision reason, the culpability reason, the similarity reason, the publication reason, and the rain-dance reason.

3   Answers will vary, but keep in mind that standardized tests *can* provide some useful (albeit limited) information about students. Other possible sources of information include observations of students' day-to-day performance in the classroom; portfolios of students' work; and assessment of students' performance on a variety of creative and practical projects.

4   Answers will vary, but some of the practices that tend to encourage development of analytic thinking and to discourage the development of creative and practical thinking include the following: frequent use of questions and activities that strongly favor analytic ways of thinking; lack of student choice in pursuing projects and ideas of interest to the student; and overreliance on standardized testing and tests that primarily involve only one "right" answer.

**5** These processes include problem identification, process selection, representation of information, strategy formation, allocation of resources, solution monitoring, and evaluating solutions. Most of these processes are measured only indirectly, if at all, by typical standardized tests.

**6** Answers will vary.

## GOAL 1: SUGGESTED READINGS

Sternberg, R. J. (1980b). Sketch of a componential subtheory of human intelligence. *The Behavioral and Brain Sciences*, 3, 573–614.

Sternberg, R. J. (1981b). Intelligence as thinking and learning skills. *Educational Leadership*, 39, 18–20.

Sternberg, R. J. (1985a). *Beyond IQ: A triarchic theory of human intelligence*. New York: Cambridge University Press.

# goal 2

## Understanding Teaching Strategies
## to Enhance Thinking

Teachers teach their students by what they do as well as by what they say. For instance, when one of the coauthors was taking courses to become a certified teacher, she took one particularly memorable course on methods for teaching mathematics. The professor in the course repeatedly admonished the students never to give children rote memorization tasks because such tasks are meaningless and a waste of time. Rather, children need to be provided with hands-on experiences that will help them truly understand mathematical concepts.

Unfortunately, the most memorable thing about the course was not what the professor intended the students to learn. Instead, it was the way that the professor would give lists of math programs and names of textbooks to memorize before every exam.

We use this anecdote to make a point about the importance of the implicit messages teachers send to students. In the mathematical methods course, the explicit message the professor gave was that rote memorization is meaningless. However, because she emphasized rote memorization on exams, she sent an implicit message that seriously undermined her explicit one. The anecdote also serves as an illustration of the multiple ways in which college professors in teacher-preparation programs, as well as staff developers in school districts, train staff. Staff developers train teachers and administrators not only through explicit messages, but also by example.

In recent years, the teaching of thinking skills has become a major area of interest for educators. Here we discuss what we believe to be one important consideration in teaching thinking, namely, teaching strategy. One reason teaching strategy is important is that, by adopting a certain strategy, the teacher models a certain role for students. This role modeling conveys, sometimes unwittingly, implicit messages to students. If the messages are of the wrong kind, then the teaching may not only be ineffective, it may actually be harmful. In some instances, the explicit message may even contradict an implicit one (e.g., as in our anecdote about the mathematical-methods course, or when a teacher encourages students to give their opinions on an issue and then shoots down opinions unlike his or her own).

## THREE ALTERNATIVE TEACHING STRATEGIES

Consider three teaching strategies and examples (Spear & Sternberg, 1987). Each of these strategies can be applied in classroom interactions, as well as in formulating homework questions, writing assignments, and projects.

## Descriptions

The first strategy is lecture-based or *didactic*. The teacher simply presents the material to be learned; there is very little teacher–student interaction, except perhaps for an occasional question from a student requesting clarification, or an occasional question from the teacher. In addition, there is no interaction among students, at least not any interaction relevant to the topic at hand. This strategy tends to favor critical–analytical thinkers like Alice (see Goal 1).

The second strategy is a *fact-based questioning approach*. The teacher asks the students many questions, which are designed primarily to elicit facts. The feedback from the teacher revolves primarily around responses such as "right," "good," "yes," and "no." In this strategy, there is much teacher–student interaction, but the interaction tends to be brief and follow-up to individual questions is generally limited. Just as in the didactic strategy, there is little or no student–student interaction unless it is "covert interaction," such as about what to wear to the dance on Saturday night. This strategy also tends to favor Alice-type thinkers.

The third strategy is the one that we argue is usually the most appropriate for the teaching of thinking skills. This strategy can be characterized as a *thinking-based questioning approach,* or simply as a *dialogical* approach, because it encourages dialogue between teacher and student, and between student and student. The dialogue may be either oral or written. In this strategy, the teacher asks questions to stimulate thinking and discussion. There is generally no one right answer to these questions, so feedback like "right" or "wrong" is generally not given. Instead, the teacher tends to comment on or add to what students have said, and may even change stance on an issue to play the devil's advocate. If the discussion rambles too far afield, the teacher may make comments or ask questions that serve to focus the discussion. Thus, in this strategy, distinctions between student and teacher tend to blur, and the teacher becomes more of a guide or a facilitator, rather than a teacher in the traditional sense. Unlike the fact-based questioning strategies, the dialogical strategy has a lot of follow-up to individual questions. There also is much more interaction among students with the dialogical strategy than with the other teaching strategies. This strategy tends to favor equally thinkers like Alice (critical–analytical), Barbara (creative–synthetic), and Celia (practical–contextual). These three strategies are summarized in Table 3.

| Table 3 | Characteristics and Uses of Three Different Teaching Strategies | | |
| --- | --- | --- | --- |
| Name | Characteristics | Best Used for | Example |
| Didactic (Lecture-based) | Teacher presents material in a lecture format. | Presenting new information. | TEACHER: "Today I'm going to tell you about the French Revolution." |
| | Minimal teacher–student and student–student interaction. | | |
| Fact-based questioning | Teacher asks questions designed primarily to elicit facts. | Reinforcing newly learned information. | TEACHER: "When did the French Revolution take place? Who were king and queen at the time?" |
| | Teacher gives "right" and "wrong" feedback. | Testing students' knowledge. | |

Table 3 | Continued

| Name | Characteristics | Best Used for | Example |
|---|---|---|---|
| | Much teacher–student interaction, but limited follow-up to individual questions. | | |
| | Minimal student–student interaction. | Bridge between didactic and dialogical strategies. | |
| Dialogical (Thinking-based questioning) | Teacher asks questions designed to stimulate thinking and discussion. | Encouraging class-discussion. | TEACHER: "How were the French Revolution and the American Revolution alike? How were they different?" |
| | Teacher gives feedback that focuses or comments on discussion. | Stimulating critical thinking. | |
| | Much teacher–student and student–student interaction. | | |

## Examples

As an example of the didactic (lecture based) teaching strategy, consider the following hypothetical presentation in a high school history class, involving the teacher and a student whom we shall call Lisa:

**Teacher**: Yesterday in class, we started talking about the French Revolution. Recall that the revolution began in 1789 with the storming of the Bastille, and that Louis XVI and Marie Antoinette were king and queen at that time. The king and queen were imprisoned and later executed by guillotine, the mode of execution strongly associated with the French Revolution.

So, in the revolution, the monarchy was overthrown, and a republic was eventually established. However, there were several years of bloodshed before the new republic actually began to take shape. During the Reign of Terror, thousands of French citizens were executed because of supposed "crimes against the people" they had committed. These executions occurred on a daily basis and were carried out with great speed. By way of example, I'll tell you about something I saw when I was in Paris last summer. I visited an historical museum, the Carnavalet, which contains many artifacts of the revolution. One of these artifacts was an order of execution, which was simply a form that had to be filled in by the judges. There were blanks for the prisoner's name, for the specific crime he or she had supposedly committed, and for the date and place of execution. Well, all of the blanks were filled in on the order of execution I saw at the Carnavalet, but what struck me was the word filled in next to the space for "date of execution." It was the French word "aujour-d'hui." Does anybody know what that means?

**Lisa**: It means "today."

**Teacher**: Right.

(*Laughter.*)

Now consider the second teaching strategy, fact-based questioning. The following hypothetical interaction involves the teacher and four students, whom we shall call David, Joan, Debbie, and Andrew.

**Teacher**: Let's review some things you've learned about the French Revolution. When did the revolution take place?

**David**: 1789.

**Teacher**: Right, that's when it began. What was happening in America at that time?

**Andrew**: The American Revolution?

**Teacher**: No . . . when did the American Revolution begin?

**Andrew**: Um . . . 17 . . .

**Joan**: 1776?

**Teacher**: Right. And it ended in 1781. So the American Revolution was already over when the French Revolution began in 1789. The Americans were no longer a British colony. In our country, we celebrate the Fourth of July as our Independence Day. What day do the French celebrate?

**David**: July fourteenth.

**Teacher**: Yes . . . what happened on that day?

**Debbie**: Bastille Day,

**Teacher**: What's that? What was the Bastille?

**Debbie**: It was a fortress used as a prison.

**Teacher**: Right. And the common people had come to identify the Bastille as a symbol of the monarchy of the king and queen. And who were the king and queen?

**Andrew**: Oh . . . Louis the Fourteenth.

**Teacher**: No, he came earlier. This was Louis the Sixteenth. Do you remember the queen's name, Andrew?

**Andrew**: Marie Antoinette.

**Teacher**: Good. So, let's get back to the Bastille. What actually happened on Bastille Day?

**David**: The people stormed the Bastille.

**Teacher**: What does that mean, that they "stormed" it?

**David**: They broke into it. They took it over.

**Teacher**: Yes. Would you be able to visit the Bastille today, to walk around inside it?

**Joan**: No. The people tore it apart. It's not there any more.

**Teacher**: Right. They took the prison apart, stone by stone. So today you could see models of the Bastille, or the place where it once stood, but the prison itself is no longer there.

Finally, consider the third teaching strategy, dialogical (thinking-based questioning). The following hypothetical interaction involves the teacher and the same four students from the previous interaction.

**Teacher**: Yesterday, we talked a little bit about how the American Revo-

**Teacher**: lution and the French Revolution were alike. But how were the two revolutions different?

**Debbie**: The French Revolution was bloodier.

**Teacher**: In what way? Both revolutions were violent; people got killed fighting them.

**Andrew**: But in the French Revolution, there was the Reign of Terror.

**Debbie**: Yeah, in the Reign of Terror, a lot of innocent people were guillotined.

**Teacher**: But some innocent people were killed in the American Revolution, too, weren't they?

**Debbie**: This was worse.

**Andrew**: Yeah, a lot of people died in the Reign of Terror.

**David**: And French people were killing their own people in the Reign of Terror. That didn't happen in the American Revolution. The Americans were killing the British, but not each other.

**Joan**: That's not true. Some colonists died fighting with the British, or because they were loyal to the British.

**David**: But getting killed in a battle isn't the same as a planned execution. And a lot of these people were executed without a trial—they'd be accused of something, and then right away, they'd have their heads chopped off, when they might not have done anything wrong.

**Andrew**: Yeah.

**Teacher**: Ah, I see. So one way that the two revolutions differed was that in the Reign of Terror of the French Revolution, a large number of people were executed by the state, often without benefit of a trial. That didn't happen in America. How else were the two revolutions different?

**Joan:** America was a British colony. We were fighting for independence from the British.

**Debbie:** Right. France wasn't a colony. France had colonies.

**Teacher:** Both revolutions involved rebellion against a monarchy, though . . . rebelling against the Crown.

**Joan:** But in France, the king was a French king . . . George the Third wasn't an American king, he was British.

**Teacher:** So the two revolutions were alike in that they both involved rebelling against a monarchy, but they were different in that America was a colony, and France wasn't. The Americans were rebelling against a foreign king, and the French were rebelling against their own king.

Although we chose history as the content vehicle for our examples of teaching strategies, one can imagine the previous interactions occurring in virtually any content area, from biology to mathematics, to foreign languages. With this book we have included examples of fact-based questions and thinking-based questions involving several different types of content: children's literature (*Charlotte's Web* by E. B. White, 1952), science (a unit on dinosaurs), and American history (a unit on the Civil War). Of course, like all of the activities included with this book, these questions should serve as a starting point for discussion rather than as passive seatwork.

## Selecting a Preferred Strategy

We maintain that one of the three teaching strategies best lends itself to promoting students' higher order thinking skills. At the same time, there are often a number of factors that teachers must consider when selecting a teaching strategy.

### The Usefulness of Each Teaching Strategy

We argue that the dialogical strategy is generally best suited to the teaching of higher order thinking for a couple of reasons. First, it is the only strategy that demands real thought from students, rather than simply spitting back answers from a book or a lecture. It's not that the other strategies cannot be thought-provoking or lead to higher order thinking, but rather that the dialogical strategy, if done properly, demands thought, rather than merely permitting it. Second, in the dialogical strategy, the teacher is serving as the best role model of what it is that he or she wants the students to do—that is, to think critically.

It is important to realize that each of the three strategies can be done well or poorly. For instance, the didactic strategy can be informative and entertaining, or uninteresting and dull. Fact-based questioning can help to test, clarify, and organize the student's knowledge, or it can be intimidating and can cut off discussion. The dialogical strategy can stimulate thinking, or it can be unfocused and confusing.

It is especially important to note that the dialogical strategy should not be a substitute for lack of preparation on the part of the teacher. In fact, if done well, the dialogical strategy is at least as demanding in terms of preparation as are the other two strategies because it requires not only that the teacher have a solid knowledge base in the content area, but also that the teacher really think about which questions should be posed to students. Moreover, the teacher needs to be highly skilled at managing group discussions. Consider, for example, the youngster who answers the question "Why do you think E. B. White called his book *Charlotte's Web*?" by responding, "Because it's about Charlotte." In this situation, the teacher needs to be able to follow up with further questions that encourage students to think more deeply about the ways that the character of Charlotte is central to the book.

The point should also be made that each strategy has a place in teaching. We are not claiming that all instruction should take place via the dialogical strategy, nor even that this strategy is necessarily the preferred mode of instruction. Indeed, although we have presented prototypes of three different teaching strategies for the purpose of this discussion, in real life, teaching strategies are generally some interwoven combination of the strategies we have presented here, with strategy shifting as teachers shift objectives.

Which strategy is "best" depends at least partly on what the teacher aims to accomplish in a particular situation. The didactic strategy is useful for imparting knowledge—for presenting information that is new to the audience. Students cannot have a dialogical-strategy discussion concerning a topic about which they have no information.

The fact-based questioning strategy is useful for reinforcing newly learned information, for guiding student thinking, and for helping the teacher to discover gaps in student knowledge. This strategy may also serve as a sort of bridge between the didactic teaching strategy and the dialogical one.

If students have never been required to do much thinking or to engage in much discussion, then abruptly demanding these things from them may be too intimidating. Fact-based questioning might then serve as a more gradual way of leading into the dialogical strategy. To return to the *Charlotte's Web* question as an example, when asked why E. B. White chose this particular title, many students might not be able to come up with any response at all; rather, they might simply shrug and say, "I don't know." The teacher might then pose some fact-based questions that lead gradually into more thinking-based questions about the title: Who was Charlotte? How did she help Wilbur? How is she important in the book? Nevertheless, for reasons we have already discussed, the dialogical strategy is preferred for stimulating higher order thinking and for encouraging class discussion, especially discussion involving interaction among students as well as interaction between student and teacher.

## Other Factors to Consider

Teaching strategy interacts with a number of important factors, including the teacher's personality, students' preference for a particular strategy of teaching, and the nature of the subject matter. First consider the factor of teacher personality, which tends to lead the teacher to prefer one strategy over another. One of the authors is well-acquainted with a teacher who is a particularly outstanding lecturer. This person puts a great deal of time and effort into writing lectures, and is so entertaining that she is extremely popular with students. This teacher has even commented privately that she had a secret ambition to be a comedienne or an actress, and this ambition was satisfied, in a way she had not originally anticipated, by teaching. Clearly, this individual's personality has led her to a preference for the didactic strategy, and it is a strategy she carries off superbly. However, in order to adopt another strategy, particularly the dialogical one, she would have to relinquish a certain amount of control over her audience. Moreover, she would need to accept a certain blurring of the distinction in roles between herself and her students. These are things she seems unwilling or unable to do.

Second, just as teachers may have a personal preference for one strategy over another, students may have a preference for a particular teaching strategy. We have already suggested that past experience may predispose students toward a particular teaching strategy. For example, students who are used to the didactic strategy may initially find the dialogical one intimidating, or may not know how to respond.

Furthermore, students have certain preferred strategies of learning, just as teachers have certain preferred strategies of teaching. Thus, a student's preferred strategy of learning leads him or her to a preferred strategy of instruction from the teacher. For instance, students who are creative and who enjoy generating their own ideas and projects might well have a natural inclination toward the dialogical strategy. On the other hand, students who are do-ers—who like to carry out the ideas and projects that have been generated by themselves or by others—might be more inclined toward one of the other teaching strategies.

We do not advocate the use of only one teaching strategy. For one thing, students need exposure to a variety of strategies in order to develop a variety of skills. If they are never exposed to the dialogical strategy, for instance, and they are never required to engage in the kind of discussion that demands thinking, their ability to think may be impaired. Furthermore, exclusive use of one strategy, whether it be lecture or discussion, tends to become boring.

Overreliance on one strategy to the exclusion of the others probably makes for less effective instruction than does use of alternating strategies. Even when using the lecture format (the didactic strategy), the teacher needs to ask some fact-based questions, if only to find out which points require further clarification. And even in situations ideally suited to a dialogical strategy, teachers need to guide, summarize, and clarify in a way that draws upon the other teaching strategies.

By now one thing should be clear to you, the reader, just as it was to Socrates, the Greek philosopher and master teacher: Nothing is more critical to the development of dialogue and ultimately to the development of thinking than are the questioning strategies the teacher uses and teaches the students to use for themselves. In the next section, we consider alternative ways of teaching students to ask and answer questions.

## SUMMARY

In this goal, we have described three teaching strategies: didactic, fact-based questioning, and dialogical. In the didactic strategy, one directly presents material to the students for them immediately to learn. In the fact-based questioning strategy, one asks questions of fact, with right and wrong answers. And in the dialogical strategy, one encourages students to question themselves and to arrive at answers, which are usually not of the right-or- wrong variety. Good teaching involves a mix of all three strategies.

## GOAL 2: SELF-DIRECTED QUESTIONS AND ACTIVITIES

**1** Describe three alternative teaching strategies and how each may be especially useful.

**2** Which of the three strategies do you prefer as a teacher? Why? As a student? Why?

**3** Ask a colleague who understands the differences among the three teaching strategies to observe you and to record which strategies you rely upon across several subjects. (You can also try to keep track of these strategies on your own if such a colleague is unavailable.) Then try to implement the dialogical strategy more often in at least one domain where you previously were using it very little or not at all.

**4** After you have carried out the implementation in #3, answer the following questions. What were some of the benefits of using the dialogical strategy? Were there problems with using it? How might these problems be addressed?

**1** Three alternative teaching strategies are the didactic strategy, which may be particularly useful for introducing new information; the fact-based questioning strategy, which may be particularly useful for uncovering gaps in students' knowledge and for guiding students toward a dialogical strategy; and the dialogical strategy, which we have argued is most useful for developing students' higher order thinking skills.

**2** Answers will vary, but many teachers rely too heavily on a didactic strategy in teaching. However, one may prefer a different strategy as a student than as a teacher. For example, teachers who are very didactic in their own teaching sometimes prefer a dialogical strategy when they themselves are students.

**3** Answers will vary.

**4** Answers will vary, but keep in mind that a dialogical strategy can be very challenging to implement, especially if one has not previously been using it. Students may initially resist the strategy and teachers may have difficulty carrying off the strategy well. Usually these problems diminish with time and effort.

## Goal 2: Teaching Activities

### *Charlotte's Web*

**Fact-Based Questions:**

1. What did Mr. Arable plan to do to Wilbur when he was first born? Why?

2. Who was Templeton?

3. What did Charlotte do to save Wilbur's life?

4. How did Wilbur get Charlotte's egg sac back to Zuckerman's farm?

**Thinking-Based Questions:**

1. Why do you think E. B. White called his book *Charlotte's Web*? (Why, for example, didn't he call it *Wilbur* or *Zuckerman's Farm*?)

2. In your opinion, would the book have had a better ending if Charlotte had not died at the end of it? Why or why not?

3. What kind of character was Templeton? Did you like him? Why or why not?

### Dinosaurs

**Fact-Based Questions:**

1. When did the dinosaurs live?

2. Give at least three examples of different kinds of dinosaurs.

3. What kinds of food did the dinosaurs eat?

4. What was Tyrannosaurus rex?

*Thinking-Based Questions:*

1. What are some reasons why dinosaurs might have become extinct?

2. Although many scientists think that dinosaurs were related to modern reptiles, other scientists have argued that dinosaurs might have been related to birds.

How are dinosaurs like reptiles?

How are they like birds?

Do they seem more like birds or like reptiles to you?

## The American Civil War

*Fact-Based Questions:*

1. When did the Civil War take place?

2. What event officially started the war?

3. Which battles marked a turning point in the war in favor of the Union?

4. What happened at Appomattox?

5. Who was John Wilkes Booth?

*Thinking-Based Questions:*

1. Imagine that you are a Confederate soldier from Georgia. What arguments might you make to defend the right of Georgia to secede from the Union and join the Confederacy?

2. How might America's history have been changed if Lincoln had not been assassinated?

3. Are the events of the Civil War still influencing modern-day America? If so, how? If not, why not?

## Goal 2: Answer Key

### *Charlotte's Web*

**Answers to Fact-Based Questions**

1. Mr. Arable planned to kill Wilbur because he was the runt of the litter.

2. A rat.

3. She spun messages about Wilbur into her web.

4. He carried it in his mouth.

### Dinosaurs

**Answers to Fact-Based Questions**

1. Millions of years ago.

2. Some examples are Apatosaurus, Tyrannosaurus, Stegosaurus, Deinonychus, and Triceratops.

3. Some dinosaurs ate meat whereas others ate only plants.

4. Tyrannosaurus was among the largest meat-eating dinosaur.

### The American Civil War:

**Answers to Fact-Based Questions**

1. 1861–1865.

2. Beauregard's order to fire upon Fort Sumter (South Carolina) officially began the war.

3. The Union victories at Gettysburg and Vicksburg.

4. Lee formally surrendered to Grant.

5. President Lincoln's assassin.

## GOAL 2: SUGGESTED READINGS

Baron, J. B., & Sternberg, R. J. (Eds.). (1987). *Teaching thinking skills: Theory and practice*. New York: Freeman.

Nickerson, R. S., Perkins, D. N., & Smith, E. E. (1985). *Teaching thinking*. Hillsdale, NJ: Erlbaum.

Whimbey, A., & Whimbey, L. S. (1975). *Intelligence can be taught*. New York: E. P. Dutton.

# goal 3

## Understanding the Role of Questioning
### in Developing Thinking Skills

One of the best ways to teach dialogically is to encourage children to ask questions (Sternberg, 1994a). Children are natural question-askers: They have to be to learn how to adapt to a complex and changing environment. But whether they continue to ask questions—and especially, to ask good questions—depends in large part on how adults *respond* to their questions. The ability to ask good questions and to know how to answer them is an essential part of intelligence, arguably the most important part (Arlin, 1990; Getzels &

Csikszentmihalyi, 1976; Sternberg, 1985b). It is an ability that we can either foster or stifle.

Lev Vygotsky (1978) proposed that a primary means by which people develop intelligence is *internalization*. We incorporate into ourselves what we absorb from the environment. Reuven Feuerstein (1980) referred to a primary example of this process as *mediated learning experience*. The parent as teacher helps the child make sense of the environment by providing guidance to the child in how to interpret it. Feuerstein suggested that children who show deficient intellectual skills are often those who have been exposed to insufficient mediation of their learning experiences. In this view, it is not enough just to take the child to a museum or to see interesting sites. What is important is the mediation of the experience for the child by the parent or teacher. In Piagetian (1972) terms, such mediation helps children assimilate new experiences into existing schemas and accommodate more novel experiences through the formation of new schemas.

When children seek such mediation by asking questions, parents and teachers have characteristic ways of responding. Our argument here is that these characteristic ways of responding can be divided into seven levels, with higher levels representing superior mediation and thus superior opportunities for the child to develop his or her higher order thinking skills (Sternberg, 1994a). In other words, the basic idea is that mediators—usually parents or teachers—who respond to questions at higher levels are better at fostering the intellectual development of children. Furthermore, once they understand this basic idea, mediators can put it to use immediately.

Consider as an example a question that arose when one of us visited Holland recently: Why are people in Holland so tall? For the first time in the author's life, he felt short. What's behind the considerable height of so many Dutch people? Let's consider the various levels of responses that this question and others like it might provoke.

*Level 1: Rejection of questions.* When mediators respond

at this level, the basic message to the child is to shut up. Questions are seen as inappropriate or as irritating. Children should learn to "be seen and not heard," and to keep their place. The result of consistent punishment for asking questions is, of course, that children learn not to ask questions. Hence, they learn not to learn.

Everyone would probably like to believe that he or she would never respond to children's questions at such a low and even offensive level. Perhaps one hears parents on the bus or in the subway treat children like this, but one would never do so oneself. Yet we believe that only a most unusual parent or teacher does not occasionally lapse into such behavior, if only from exhaustion.

*Level 2: Restatement of questions as responses.* At this level, the mediator answers the children's questions, but in a wholly empty way. Responses are nothing more than restatements of the original questions. So one says that people from Holland are tall because they are Dutch, or that a person acts a certain way "because he's human" or acts crazy "because he is insane." Or one says that some people come up with good solutions "because they are high in intelligence." Often mediators are not even aware that they are restating a question, because they have a highfalutin but empty word that hides their ignorance.

*Level 3: Admission of ignorance or presentation of information.* A Level 3 response to a question can be given either with or without reinforcement. An unreinforced Level 3 response—probably the most common type of answer one gives to children—consists of either saying that one does not know or giving a direct answer on the basis of what one does know. Children are thus given the opportunity to understand that their adult mediators do not know everything and are given the opportunity to learn something new. Such answers are quite reasonable in certain situations, but they do not represent the best that parents and teachers can do for children. (By the way, answering as though you know the answer when you really do not is not a response at any of these levels; it's just plain stupid because it gives children wrong information and teaches them to pretend to possess knowledge they do not really have).

The only difference between unreinforced and reinforced Level 3 responses is that in the latter case the mediator precedes the response with a reinforcing statement, such as "That's a good question" or "I'm glad you asked that." Such a response rewards question asking and is likely to increase its frequency, thereby fostering further opportunities for children to learn.

*Level 4: Encouragement to seek response through authority.* Level 4 responses fall into two categories, depending on whether the mediator takes responsibility for consulting authoritative opinions or offers that opportunity to the child. At Level 4 the process of responding to a question does not just end with an answer or an admission of ignorance. Children are taught that information can be sought out. If the parent or teacher takes responsibility for looking up the answer, children will learn that information can be sought but that someone else should do the seeking. Thus the learning that will ultimately be accomplished is *passive* learning. If children are offered the opportunity to find the information themselves—whether in an encyclopedia, a textbook, a topical book, or other reference—they assume the responsibility for their own learning. Hence they learn to learn in an *active* mode. They develop their own information-seeking skills, rather than just being given the information they seek.

*Level 5: Consideration of alternative explanations.* At this level, the mediator indicates his or her uncertainty as to the response, but suggests some alternatives and invites the child to consider which might be correct. For example, an adult might suggest that Dutch people are tall because of diet, weather, genetics, hormonal injections, the murder of short children, the wearing of elevator shoes, and so on. The child thus comes to realize that even seemingly simple questions can invite serious hypothesizing. Or an adult mediator might encourage a child to generate alternative explanations, perhaps in collaboration with the adult. Once again, learning of this kind is more *active* than merely considering alternatives generated by an adult.

*Level 6: Consideration of explanations plus means of evaluating them.* At this level, students are encouraged not only to generate alternatives, but to reflect on methods for comparing these alternatives. For example, if genetics were responsible for the high average height of the Dutch, what might one expect to observe? How might one discern whether food or weather is responsible? How can one quickly rule out the possibility that the Dutch kill short children? Through the responses of their mediators, children can see not only how to generate alternative hypotheses, but also how to test them.

*Level 7: Consideration of explanations plus means of evaluating and follow-through on evaluations.* In Level 7 the mediator actually encourages the child to perform the experiments that could distinguish among the alternative explanations. The child learns not only how to think, but how to act upon his or her thoughts. Although it may not be possible to test every explanation of a phenomenon, it will often be possible to test several of them. For example, the child can observe whether taller Dutch parents also tend to have taller children, whether there are reports of missing short children, and so on.

Note how the levels go from rejecting children's questions, at one extreme, to encouraging hypothesis formation and testing, at the other. The levels go from no learning, to passive rote learning, to analytic and creative learning, as well as practical learning. By questioning at Level 7, one equally promotes the development of critical–analyitical thinkers (like Alice), creative–synthetic thinkers (like Barbara), and practical–contextual thinkers (like Celia; see Goal 1). Parents probably do not have the time or resources to give children Level 7 responses every time they ask a question. However, when people talk about effects of socioeconomic class on intelligence, we believe people are at least partly talking about one variable that may be hiding the effects of one or more others. In other words, socioeconomic class may, in effect, be a proxy for a large number of other variables, such as health status, nutrition, opportunities, rearing environment, and so on. Children of higher socioeconomic status seem to receive, on average, higher level responses from parents to their questions (see Heath, 1983). But the higher level strategies described here are ones that can be used by teachers in any classroom and by parents at any economic level.

We have provided two examples of activities designed to encourage children to formulate hypotheses and to test them. One activity (*The Weather*) involves science content and the other (*My Community*) involves social-studies content. In these activities, children first are asked to generate several questions about each topic, then to select one question to pursue further. Many children may be inclined to generate and to pursue trivial or easy questions, so it is important for the teacher to encourage them toward questions that are interesting and challenging. Of course, like the other activities in this book, these may be adapted to suit a variety of situations and content domains.

We believe that one of the single most helpful things parents and teachers can do to help children develop their intelligence is a simple one: take children's questions seriously, and turn these questions into golden opportunities to think and learn. Ultimately, that is the goal of the dialogical method developed by Socrates. But teaching children to ask good questions has to be embedded in a strong overall plan for teaching the children to think. We will consider this overall plan next.

## SUMMARY

In this goal, we have described seven different strategies for helping children to develop questioning and answering techniques. The strategies are hierarchically arranged, with strategies higher in the hierarchy (later strategies) generally promoting thinking more than do strategies lower in the hierarchy (earlier strategies). But teachers need to use their judgment for when to use which strategies. What is important is that they give students opportunities, whenever possible, to develop questioning as well as answering skills.

1 Think of a question that you have recently been asked by a student. Imagine seven possible responses to the question, from least to most desirable, based upon the seven levels of response discussed in the text.

2 Pair up with a colleague. Take turns observing each other's teaching and record the kinds of responses that you each tend to give to questions. Then discuss some ways that you might alter these responses to develop students' thinking skills better.

**1** Answers will vary, but the seven levels are: rejection of question; restatement of questions as responses; admission of ignorance or presentation of information; encouragement to seek response through authority; consideration of alternative explanations; consideration of explanations plus means of evaluating them; and finally, consideration of explanations plus means of evaluating and follow-through on evaluation.

**2** Answers will vary. Obviously, it is not possible to answer every question with a level 7 response. In general, however, we have argued that higher level kinds of responses are better for developing students' thinking skills than are lower level kinds of responses. It is also important to expose *all* students—low achievers as well as high achievers—to some higher level kinds of responses.

## Goal 3: Teaching Activities

### The Weather

1. List as many facts as you can that you already know about weather.

2. What are some things that you do not know about the weather or about some aspect of weather—such as storms, rain, snow, and so on—that you would like to find out? List these things as questions.

3. Pick the question from #2 that you think is most interesting. Try to suggest some *possible* answers to the question.

4. What could you do to find out whether any of the possibilities in #3 is correct? For example, what are some places to find information about the weather? Are there people who can provide information? Are there observations you can make or experiments you can do?

5. Follow through to find out the answer to your question.

### My Community

1. Summarize what you already know about your community (for example, its size, location, and history).

2. What are some things that you do not know about your community that you would like to find out? List these things as questions.

3. Pick the question from #2 that you think is most interesting. Try to suggest some *possible* answers to the question.

4. What could you do to find out whether any of the possibilities in #3 is correct? For example, what are some places to find information about your community? Are there people who can provide information? Are there observations you can make or experiments you can do?

5. Follow through to find out the answer to your question.

## GOAL 3: SUGGESTED READINGS

Arlin, P. K. (1990). Wisdom: The art of problem finding. In R. J. Sternberg (Ed.), *Wisdom: Its nature, origins, and development* (pp. 230–243). New York: Cambridge University Press.

Chipman, S., Siegel, J., & Glaser, R. (Eds.). (1985). *Thinking and learning skills: Current research and open questions* (Vol. 2). Hillsdale, NJ: Erlbaum.

Lipman, M., Sharp, A. M., & Oscanyan F. S. (1980). *Philosophy in the classroom* (2nd ed.). Philadelphia: Temple University Press.

# goal 4

## Teaching the Three Ways of Thinking

As teachers we often find ourselves wondering why so few, if any, of the techniques of instruction and evaluation we use, work for everyone, or even almost everyone. If we ask students in a literature class, for example, to analyze a character's motives, some pupils may take to the assignment like fish to water, and others seem to feel lost at sea. If we ask them to write a short story, a different group of people may take to the assignment. And if we ask the same class how they could apply what they have learned in a literature lesson to their everyday lives, still another group of pupils may respond. The same divergences occur in any subject. For example, in science, some pupils take to solving problems from a textbook, others to doing independent projects, and still others to applying principles of science to everyday life, or through technology.

There can be any number of reasons why nothing works for everyone. But almost certainly, one of the most important reasons is that students, and everyone else, have multiple abilities, or intelligences, and almost any single approach to instruction and evaluation will tend to favor certain patterns of abilities over others. Thus, if we wish to reach the most students possible, the way to do so is through diversification of our instruction and evaluation.

The triarchic theory of human intelligence can be immediately applied in the classroom (Sternberg, 1994b). Its application is different, however, from that of some other theories of multiple intelligences, such as Gardner's (1983), for example. Gardner's theory of multiple intelligences specifies domains of talent. Thus, it suggests *domains* or fields of human endeavor that we might wish to incorporate into our curriculum, such as musical or bodily-kinesthetic. The triarchic theory (Sternberg, 1985a), in contrast, specifies *uses* of human knowledge (i.e., for analytical, creative, or practical purposes). Thus, this theory applies in all domains and subject matter areas. An implication of this point of view is that the two theories are not incompatible; in fact, we have integrated the theories in a jointly developed program (Gardner, Krechevsky, Sternberg, & Okagaki, 1994; Sternberg, Okagaki, & Jackson, 1990; Williams, Blythe, White, Sternberg, Li, & Gardner, 1996).

Table 4 shows examples of how the theory can be applied in six subject-matter areas: art, biology, history, literature, mathematics, and psychology. These fields, of

| | Analytic | Creative | Practical |
|---|---|---|---|
| **Table 4** | Triarchic Theory Applied to Student Instruction and Assessment Methods | | |

| | Analytic | Creative | Practical |
|---|---|---|---|
| Psychology | Compare Freud's theory of dreaming to Crick's. | Design an experiment to test a theory of dreaming. | What are the implications of Freud's theory of dreaming for your life? |
| Biology | Evaluate the validity of the bacterial theory of ulcers. | Design an experiment to test the bacterial theory of ulcers. | How would the bacterial theory of ulcers change conventional treatment regimens? |
| Literature | In what ways were Catherine Earnshaw and Daisy Miller similar? | Write an alternative ending to *Wuthering Heights* uniting Catherine and Heathcliff in life. | Why are lovers sometimes cruel to each other and what can we do about it? |
| History | How did events in post-World War I Germany lead to the rise of Nazism? | How might Truman have encouraged the surrender of Japan without dropping the A-bomb? | What lessons does Nazism hold for events in Bosnia today? |
| Mathematics | How is this mathematical proof flawed? | Prove—. . . . How might catastrophe theory be applied to psychology? | How is trigonometry applied to construction of bridges? |
| Art | Compare and contrast how Rembrandt and Van Gogh used light in. . . | Draw a beam of light. | How could we reproduce the lighting in this painting in the same actual room? |

course, are only representative of those taught in school to which the theory can be applied. In addition, we have included two activities that can be copied and given directly to students: one for younger children (*Earthquakes*), and one for secondary-level students (*Othello*). Each activity involves an analytical, creative, and practical question (in that order).

When teaching and evaluating to emphasize analytical abilities (those in which Alice excels—see Goal 1), you are asking students to (a) compare and contrast, (b) analyze, (c) evaluate, (d) critique, (e) ask why, (f) explain why, (g) explain causes, (h) or evaluate assumptions. Of course, there are other prompts for analytic thinking as well.

When teaching and evaluating for creative abilities (those in which Barbara in Goal 1 excels), you are asking students to (a) create, (b) invent, (c) imagine (d) design, (e) show how, (f) suppose, or (g) say what would happen if . . . . Most teachers find that more of their instruction and evaluation is oriented toward analytic than toward creative abilities.

When teaching and evaluating to emphasize practical abilities (those in which Celia in Goal 1 excels), you are asking students to (a) apply, (b) show how they can use something, (c) implement, (d) utilize, or (e) demonstrate how in the real world . . . . Relatively little traditional instruction and evaluation is oriented toward practical abilities, which may be why children have so much difficulty applying what they learn in school to their lives outside school.

Of course, there is a fourth kind of instruction and evaluation in our schools, which is actually the kind that predominates in most classrooms. This kind asks students things like (a) who said . . . , (b) summarize, (c) who did . . . , (d) when did . . . , (e) what did . . . , (f) how did . . . , (g) repeat back . . . , and (h) describe . . . . Instruction and evaluation of this kind emphasizes what students know. Obviously, there is nothing wrong with this emphasis: Students need to acquire a knowledge base. But to the extent that you are interested in developing students' thinking skills, you need to keep in mind that, ultimately, what matters is not what you know, but how well you can use what you know—analytically, creatively, and practically.

What is important in teaching is balance: Students should be given opportunities to learn via analytical, creative, and practical thinking as well as via memory. There is no one right way to teach or learn that works for all students. By balancing types of instruction and assessment, you reach all students, not just some of them.

For example, in the *Earthquakes* activity, a creative–synthetic thinking youngster like Olivia in Goal 1 might gravitate naturally to the second question (imagining that she has been in an earthquake and writing a story about it). It is very important for Olivia to have the opportunity to exploit the creative abilities that are an obvious strength for her. But of course, Olivia should not be limited *only* to creative types of activities; rather, like all youngsters, she should be encouraged to develop analytic and practical as well as creative abilities in a balanced way.

We practice what we preach in our own teaching. In one assignment we gave to high school students taking a summer psychology course at Yale (Sternberg, 1994c), the students learned about depression. They then had to (a) compare two theories of depression (analytic), (b) synthesize their own theory of depression (creative), and (c) give advice to a hypothetical depressed friend as to how to overcome the depression (practical). The same kind of design could be used in any subject-matter area taught at any level. At the elementary level, an example might involve a topic such as whales. For example, students might be asked to compare and contrast whales versus fish (analytic), to draw a picture and write a story about whales (creative), and to think of some ways to keep whales from becoming endangered or extinct (practical). One needs to gauge the level of instruction to the level of the students being taught, but students at *any* level can think analytically, creatively, and practically. Teachers just need to give them the chance.

We used to think that large portions of our students just were not very bright when it came to the subjects we teach. When we began diversifying our instruction and assessment via the triarchic model, we discovered that many students who we thought could not do well could, if only we gave them a chance. Obviously, one cannot and should not always teach to students' strengths. Students need to learn to remedy and compensate for weaknesses, too. Teachers can help them do so by being flexible in their instruction and evaluation, namely, by teaching and assessing via the triarchic model.

## A FOUR-STEP MODEL FOR TEACHING THE THREE WAYS OF THINKING

What is a process by which we might teach the three ways of thinking we have discussed? Here we present a four-step model that provides such a process based on Sternberg and Davidson (1989). Let us start by considering the following real-world example: A family we know owns a beautiful house. Unfortunately, the house is covered with innumerable brown bugs. The bugs are called box-elder bugs, and they have flown onto the house from a nearby tree. The tree, called a box-elder tree, is considered a public nuisance. The owners of the house wish to rid the house of the bugs, especially because the bugs start to infiltrate the house in cold weather. The problem: How can the owners get rid of the bugs?

The son suggests cutting down the tree. The husband asks the family if there are any potential problems with this solution. The daughter points out that the tree might fall on the house if it is cut down. The wife suggests that there may be other box-elder trees in the neighborhood, so that cutting down one tree will not get rid of the bugs; they may fly to the house from the other trees. The husband observes that it is not clear that the tree is on their own property. As it turns out, the tree is, in fact, on a neighbor's property. The son suggests cutting down the tree at night, but the rest of the family vetoes this idea.

The daughter suggests calling the exterminators to poison the bugs. The wife remembers how they had used a similar solution in trying to get rid of carpenter ants. But the son points out a problem: Won't the bugs come back, sooner or later? The wife observes that this was, in fact, what happened with the carpenter ants.

The husband suggests consulting an expert entomologist. This solution was tried, and the entomologist suggested "learning to love the bugs." He did not know how to get rid of them either.

The family also considers moving. However, this solution seems to be an expensive one; and they are not sure they could sell their present house, given its unappealing appearance.

Finally, the wife notices that not all of the other houses in the neighborhood have box-elder bugs. The family spends some time trying to figure out what might distinguish the houses that have the bugs from those that do not. Finally, they hit on the correct answer. All the houses that have the bugs are painted white or painted in a very light color. None of the houses without bugs are painted in a light color. The solution (which was that actually employed by the victims of the bugs) is to paint the house brown.

This scenario illustrates some of the processes employed in a four-step model for intellectual-skills development that has been used successfully in teaching a variety of intellectual skills at various levels of schooling. Indeed, the model derived from our work in teaching such skills (Davidson & Sternberg, 1984; Sternberg, 1986). Our purpose here is to describe the model and how it can be implemented in school settings. The four prongs of the model are (a) familiarization, (b) intragroup problem solving, (c) intergroup problem solving, and (d) individual problem solving.

## Familiarization

Familiarization comprises a set of instructional procedures for conveying thinking skills. Consider in more detail just what we mean.

*Presentation and interactive solution in real-world problems.* The first element involves presenting a set of two or three real-world problems and working together with the students as a group to solve these problems. These problems may come from a book on thinking skills (such as Bransford & Stein, 1993, or Sternberg, 1986), from the subject matter of the particular course, from newspapers, or from people's everyday lives. We have included two examples of "everyday" problems that teachers can use with students: *The Briarwood Park* problem (for elementary children), and *The Central City High School Problem* (for secondary students). The purpose of this phase of instruction is to motivate students to view the to-be-taught skills as life-relevant and to set the stage for the application of the skills to everyday life. In thinking through the box-elder problem with little assistance from the teacher, students learn how to approach problems they might face in their environment. At this point, no reference is made to any particular thinking skills, or even to the fact that the goal of the instruction is to teach thinking. It is essential that the teacher provide only the minimal structure needed to define and solve each problem. The teacher should work in a Socratic rather than a didactic mode, drawing the students out so that they both define and solve the problem, and evaluate the alternative solutions as they go along.

*Group analysis of problem-solving procedures.* Once two or three problems have been solved, the teacher suggests that students think about the mental processes and strategies they used to solve each of the problems, and then tell the group what they believe one or more of these processes or strategies to have been. For example, how did they try to solve the box-elder problem? The goal is to have the students rather than the teacher come up with the skills to be taught. Students might come up with processes such as "compare two things," "use past experiences," "make predictions," and so on. Their introspections about their own processing are usually quite accurate. The students are thereby given a stake in the outcome of the lesson. The teacher is nonevaluative and encourages students to be as introspective as possible. One does not worry about the labels used to describe thinking processes, but rather is concerned that the concepts are conveyed in a way that is clear to the other members of the class, as well as to the teacher.

*Labeling of mental processes and strategies.* Once the students have provided a fairly comprehensive list of processes and strategies, the teacher notes that the day's lesson will deal only with a subset of these processes and strategies and, moreover, that it would be useful to have a common name for the processes and strategies in order to facilitate communication among the class members. The teacher then provides the labels, showing how the labels encompass the processes and strategies that the students generated, and showing how the processes and strategies do, in fact, apply to the real-world problems that have been solved. It is important that the teacher emphasize that the labels are matters of convention to facilitate communication and that it is the set of concepts, rather than the set of labels, that is important for understanding human thought. For example, identifying exactly what the box-elder problem is (a problem of getting rid of bugs, of getting rid of a house by moving, or of modifying the house by painting) proves to be essential to the problem's solution.

*Application of labeled processes to initial problems.* The teacher now challenges the students to show how each of the newly labeled processes was used in the solution of the problems presented earlier. For example, the teacher can now speak of "identifying the problem." Through this step, the students connect their initial problem solving with the day's lesson.

*Application of labeled processes to new problems.* The teacher now presents two or three new problems, of the order of the box-elder problem, and asks the students to work together to solve these problems. However, now the students are asked to describe and label the mental processes and strategies. The labels provide verbal mediation to the students so that they better understand what they are doing, and can better communicate it to others. Thus, the students now immediately realize what they are doing as they are doing it.

*Student generation of new problems.* Finally, the students are asked to generate their own interesting and consequential problems, and then to solve them together using (among others) the mental processes and strategies forming the basis for the thinking-skills lesson. This step is crucial because it encourages students to apply their newly developed thinking skills not only to problems that are given to them by someone else, but also to problems that they face on their own, quite often outside a classroom setting. And when people are on their own, problems are almost never handed to them on a platter.

## Intragroup Problem Solving

In intragroup problem solving, the members of the class work together to solve a new problem, with no intervention at all from the teacher other than to serve as an observer of the class discussion. The teacher may choose a student to serve as a moderator for the discussion. The students are encouraged to use the processes and strategies they have just learned, as well as others, to solve the problem. The teacher may choose to comment on the group problem-solving processes, but not until the problem solving is completed. Students are encouraged to brainstorm and to be mutually supportive. We strongly believe in the importance of group problem solving, because our society, especially, places so little emphasis on it in classroom instruction but so much emphasis on it in the real world. One has only to observe the results of some foreign-policy fiascoes, such as the Bay of Pigs, or some of the results of university faculty meetings, to observe how individuals who are excellent individual problem solvers can be awful group problem solvers. The goal is to get students to work together to construct an orderly and productive protocol for group problem solving.

Williams and Sternberg (1988), in analyses of group problem solving, have used simulations for studying and developing intragroup problem-solving skills. In one problem, for example, students were given a scenario of a small town in a rural area of the state that for years had served as a retreat for people wishing to get away from it all. But now speculators were moving in, buying up land, and planning to sell it to land-developers at a profit. The land-developers, in turn, were changing the rural nature of the town and transforming it into a resort. The problem posed to the students was to come up with a plan to save the essential character of the town, while at the same time allowing for some controlled development. They were asked actually to construct the plan and write it down. In another problem, students were asked to imagine that they worked for an advertising firm attempting to create an advertising campaign for a company that has produced a sugar substitute. The sugar substitute looks like sugar, tastes like sugar, dissolves like sugar, is non-caloric, and causes cancer in some laboratory animals. The problem was to create an advertising poster that was appealing and yet honest. The students actually had to create the poster. In each of these problem-solving situations, students worked together to produce the best possible product. Again, their efforts—both the group process and product—were evaluated only after they were completed.

## Intergroup Problem Solving

The third step of the model involves intergroup problem solving. In intergroup problem solving, students work in two or more groups to come up with alternative solutions. The two groups may work independently and then compare and contrast their solutions, or be preassigned sides in an issue, as in a debate. The idea is not to encourage competition, but rather careful monitoring and evaluation of solutions. Intragroup problem solving is an excellent way to develop brain storming and cooperative skills; but sometimes groups become too cohesive, and fail to monitor the quality of their own solutions (Janis, 1972). Thus, intergroup problem solving encourages the use of the monitoring and evaluation metacomponents as well as the planning ones. Sometimes, intergroup problem solving may take the form of games, especially at the lower levels of instruction. Our experience suggests that games can be fun as well as intellectually challenging for the students. It is important that the games or contests be presented in a spirit of fun and that competition be deemphasized. The main goal should be to encourage students to do their best possible thinking as a way to help their team and themselves.

## Individual Problem Solving

In the final step of the model, individual problem solving, students are presented with problems on an individual basis, and solve them individually as well. Following a Vygotskian model of knowledge acquisition (Vygotsky, 1978), individual problem solving is generally placed after, rather than before, group problem solving. The intra- and inter-group efforts serve a social–cognitive function that enables students to internalize means of approaching and solving problems. In other words, the student is encouraged to engage within him or herself the same kinds of dialectic that he or she has observed in groups. The different aspects of the mind, like the different students, both cooperate and compete with each other to arrive at the best possible solution to a problem.

The four-step model we have proposed assumes that the teacher's goal is to teach students to be better thinkers, and to do so by engaging students in *dialogue*—with the teacher, with other students, and even with themselves. Ideally, they learn to conduct dialogues in ways that balance analytical, creative, and practical thinking skills, thereby achieving a balance in the kinds of thinking exemplified by Alice, Barbara, and Celia (see Goal 1). The concept of dialogue is crucial to the development of thinking skills. In later sections we explicitly consider how teachers can engage students in the kinds of dialogue with others and with themselves that promote all three ways of thinking. First, however, we will take a closer look at one frequently neglected area: thinking skills involving creativity and insight.

## SUMMARY

In this goal, we have described a four-prong strategy for teaching children to think. The four prongs are familiarization, in which students are oriented to a problem; intragroup problem solving, in which children work together in small groups to formulate and deal with a problem; intergroup problem solving, in which children discuss across groups how they have dealt with the problem at hand; and individual problem solving, in which children work on their own.

## GOAL 4: SELF-DIRECTED QUESTIONS AND ACTIVITIES

**1** Think of a thematic unit or topic that you will be covering with students in the near future. Generate some examples of questions or activities involving this topic that would tap analytical, creative, and practical thinking skills.

**2** Now actually try out the questions and activities that you generated in #1, and as you are doing so, try to make some of the following observations: Which students seem to excel in a given way of thinking (analytical, creative, or practical) and which seem to have the most difficulty? Do students who have difficulty in one way of thinking sometimes excel in another? Are your observations of your own students consistent with what you have read in this section? Why or why not?

**3** Outline the four steps of the model for teaching thinking skills that is described in the text. Why do the steps involving group problem solving precede the step involving individual problem solving?

**4** Which of the four steps do you think would be most difficult to implement with your own students? Why? What are some ways that you might circumvent these difficulties?

**5** Develop a plan for implementing the model in your own classroom, beginning with problems from a specific content area or from some other source. Then, if possible, actually carry out the plan.

1. Answers will vary, but questions that tap analytical thinking tend to ask students to "analyze," "critique," "explain," and so on; those tapping creative thinking might ask students to "imagine," "create," "invent," and the like; and those tapping practical thinking might use words such as "apply," "implement," or "show how you can use."

2. Because, in our view, thinking skills are multidimensional, one would not necessarily expect students who excel in one type of thinking to excel in all types. Similarly, students who have difficulty with tasks or questions tapping one way of thinking (e.g., analytical questions) might do very well with other types of tasks or questions (e.g., creative or practical questions). The goal, of course, is for all students to develop abilities in all three ways of thinking.

3. The four steps in the model are familiarization, intragroup problem solving, intergroup problem solving, and individual problem solving. Group problem solving is a useful way to introduce students to the kinds of processes and dialectic involved in solving problems. The student then is encouraged to internalize these processes by the final step of individual problem solving.

4. Answers will vary.

5. Answers will vary.

## GOAL 4: TEACHING ACTIVITIES

### Earthquakes

1. Explain what causes an earthquake and why earthquakes are more common in some parts of the world than in others.

2. Imagine that you have been in an earthquake and write a story about it. Include as much detail as you can involving what you have learned about earthquakes.

3. What kinds of things could you do to protect yourself if you were ever in an earthquake? Think about things you could do before, during, and after a quake, and outline an "earthquake preparation" plan.

### Othello

1. Analyze the character of Othello at length. For instance, does he have a "fatal flaw"? If so, what is it? If not, explain why not. Do you feel sympathetic toward him? Why or why not?

2. Some Shakespearean plays have been redone as modern stories. For example, *West Side Story* is Leonard Bernstein's modern-day "translation" of *Romeo and Juliet*. If you were going to redo *Othello* as a modern drama, how would you adapt the play? For example, what setting would you choose? Which actors and actresses would you select to play the main characters? Outline your plot, retaining the basic theme of *Othello* but changing the details to fit modern times.

3. Discuss at length how the basic theme of *Othello* is relevant to your own life. For example, have you known people who were like the main characters of the play? What have you learned from the play that you can apply to your own life?

## The Briarwood Park Problem

The children in the town of Briarwood often play in Briarwood Park. The Little League team has its baseball games in the park and there is a swing set and a sandbox for younger children. However, recently the park has been full of bees. These bees build their nests in the ground. Many children have stepped on bees by mistake and have been stung. Other children have been stung while swinging on the swings or playing ball.

A number of people have suggested ways to get rid of the bees. One person wants to spray the ground with a powerful bee-killing chemical. Someone even suggested soaking the ground with gasoline and setting it on fire. Other people say that everyone should just stay away from the playground until winter comes and the bees die naturally. Of course, this last idea does not make most of the children happy.

Do you think any of these suggestions are good ones? Why or why not? How would you solve the bee problem?

## The Center City High School Problem

Center City High School is a racially mixed school in the middle of a large city in the northeastern United States. The president of the student council traditionally gives a speech at Center City's graduation ceremony. This year, however, the student-council president has caused quite a ruckus.

This student, who is African American, wants to quote from the writings of Louis Farrakhan, the leader of the African American group Nation of Islam, as part of his graduation speech. The quotation itself, which is about the importance of responsibility among African American males, is not especially controversial. Rather, the controversy centers upon the fact that the quotation comes from Farrakhan, whom many Whites regard as racist and anti-Semitic.

The school principal, who also happens to be African American, has threatened to bar the student-council president from speaking if the Farrakhan quotation is not deleted from the speech. If the student-council president is barred from speaking, a number of his supporters plan to picket the graduation ceremonies. However, other students, and some parents, are deeply offended by the idea of quoting Farrakhan at graduation.

The controversy has worsened racial tensions at the high school. And of course, everyone is upset that, whatever happens, it looks like graduation ceremonies are going to be ruined.

What would you do to solve this problem?

## Goal 4: Answer Key

### The Briarwood Park Problem

The use of chemicals and gasoline present obvious environmental problems. Waiting for the current crop of bees to die naturally does not rule out the possibility that new larvae could hatch the following spring. The real "Briarwood Park" problem was solved by soaking the ground with a mixture of mild soap and water, a solution suggested by an entomologist.

### The Center City High School Problem

Although there is no straightforward solution to this problem, one possibility would be to convince the student-council president to select a similar quotation from a less controversial figure; another possibility would be to allow a student with an alternative point of view to speak at graduation along with the student-council president.

## GOAL 4: SUGGESTED READINGS

Bransford, J., & Stein, B. (1993). *The ideal problem solver* (2nd ed.). San Franscisco: Freeman.

Sternberg, R. J. (1988). *The triarchic mind: A new theory of human intelligence*. New York: Viking.

Sternberg, R. J. (1994c). A triarchic model for teaching and assessing students in general psychology. *General Psychologist, 30* (2), 42–48.

# goal 5

## Focusing on Teaching and Evaluating
### Creative Insight Skills

In the preceding sections, we concentrated equally on analytic, creative, and practical skills. But what we see the least of may be teaching for creative and insightful-thinking skills—the skills in which Barbara excels (see Goal 1). Those skills are our focus in this section.

# THE NATURE OF INSIGHT

People have been interested in the nature of insight for many years (see Sternberg & Davidson, 1995). It is easy to see why: Insights such as Copernicus's, that the sun rather than the earth is the center of the solar system, and Galileo's, that two objects will fall from a height at the same rate of speed regardless of their weights, constitute some of the greatest discoveries in scientific history. It would be to the advantage of us all to understand the mental processes underlying insights of these kinds.

Conventional views of insight fall into two basic camps: the *special-process* views and the *nothing-special* views. According to special-process views, insight is a process that differs in kind from ordinary types of information processing. Among these views are the ideas that insight results from extended unconscious leaps in thinking, greatly accelerated mental processing, or a short-circuiting of normal reasoning processes. These views are intuitively appealing, but seem to carry with them at least three problematical aspects.

First, they do not really pin down what insight is. Calling insight an unconscious leap or a short-circuiting leaves insight pretty much a "black box" of unknown contents. Even if one of these theories were correct, just what insight is would remain to be identified. Second, virtually all the evidence in support of these views is anecdotal rather than experimental, and for each piece of anecdotal evidence to support one of these views, there is at least one corresponding piece of evidence to refute it. Finally, the positions are probably not pinned down sufficiently, as they stand, to permit experimental tests. As a result, it is not clear that the positions could even be proven right or wrong. It is this characteristic of provability that has probably been at least in part responsible for the scarcity of research on insight.

According to the *nothing-special* views, insight is merely an extension of ordinary perceiving, recognizing, learning, and conceiving. This view, most forcefully argued by David Perkins (1981), would see past failures to identify any special processes of insight as being due to the (alleged) fact that there is no special process of insight. Insights are merely significant products of ordinary processes. We can understand the kind of frustration that would lead Perkins and others to this view: After repeated failures to identify a construct empirically, the theorist can easily be tempted to ascribe the failure to the nonexistence of the construct. One cannot find what is not there! But it is not clear that we should yet be ready to abandon the notion that there is something special about insight. Arguments for the nothing-special views have been arguments by default—because we have not identified any of these processes, we are to believe that they have no independent existence. Such arguments would be unacceptable if we were able to make a positive case for the existence of insight processes.

## THE TRIARCHIC VIEW OF INSIGHT

The view of insight that Janet Davidson and Robert Sternberg (1984) have proposed (see also Sternberg & Lubart, 1995) is that insight consists of not one, but three separate but related psychological processes:

1. *Selective encoding.* Selective encoding involves sifting out relevant information from irrelevant information. Significant problems generally present us with large amounts of information, only some of which is relevant to problem solution. For example, the facts of a legal case are usually both numerous and confusing: An insightful lawyer must figure out which of the myriad facts are relevant to principles of law. Similarly, a doctor or psychotherapist must sift out those facts that are relevant for diagnosis or treatment. Perhaps the occupation that most directly must employ selective encoding is that of the detective: In trying to figure out who has perpetrated a crime, the detective must figure out what the relevant facts are. Failure to do so may result in the detective following up on false leads, or in having no leads to follow up on at all.

2. *Selective combination.* Selective combination involves combining what might originally seem to be isolated pieces of information into a unified whole that may or may not resemble its parts. For example, the lawyer must know how the relevant facts of a case fit together to make (or break) the case. A doctor or psychotherapist must be able to figure out how to combine information about various isolated symptoms to identify a given medical (or psychological) syndrome. A detective, having collected the facts that seem relevant to the case, must determine how they fit together to point at the guilty party rather than at anyone else.

3. *Selective comparison.* Selective comparison involves relating newly acquired information to information acquired in the past. Problem solving by analogy, for example, is an instance of selective comparison: The solver realizes that new information is similar to old information in certain ways (and dissimilar from it in other ways) and uses this information better to understand the new information. For example, an insightful lawyer will relate a current case to past legal precedents; choosing the right precedent is absolutely essential. A doctor or psychotherapist relates the current set of symptoms to previous case histories in his or her own or in others' past experiences; again, choosing the right precedents is essential. A detective may have been involved in or know about a similar case where the same modus operandi was used to perpetrate a crime. Drawing an analogy to the past case may be helpful to the detective both in understanding the nature of the crime and in figuring out who did it.

The processes of insight that are being proposed here can be applied in acquiring any type of knowledge—for example, in learning new vocabulary from context. Is insight, then, really nothing at all special, but merely a mundane extension of knowledge-acquisition skills? We do not believe this to be the case. What seems to separate insightful use of selective encoding, selective combination, and selective comparison from ordinary use of these processes is the nonobviousness of how they are to be applied, or the nonobviousness of the appropriateness of their application.

By contrast, the nature of the problem in learning vocabulary from context is very clear: The task is to define the unknown word. Moreover, the kinds of clues that are useful in defining an unknown word are circumscribed in scope. Thus, with practice, the finding and use of these clues can become fairly routine. In insightful selective encoding, selective combination, and selective comparison, it is not obvious how to apply these processes, and often it is not even obvious that they are appropriate in the first place.

We therefore agree with Perkins that the processes of insight are the same as ordinary cognitive processes. However, the circumstances of their application are different. It is much more difficult to apply selective encoding, selective combination, and selective comparison in an insightful way than it is to apply them in a routine way. Thus, we do not agree with Perkins that insightful processing differs from noninsightful processing only in terms of the way the product is evaluated.

## EXAMPLES OF INSIGHT PROBLEMS INVOLVING SELECTIVE ENCODING, SELECTIVE COMBINATION, AND SELECTIVE COMPARISON

### Selective Encoding

Consider the following problem (Sternberg, 1986). As you do so, think about how selective encoding can help you to solve the problem.

> Many scientists have offered explanations for the total extinction of dinosaurs and other creatures 65 million years ago. One of the facts agreed on by most geologists is that the earth was struck by a huge asteroid or comet approximately 10 kilometers in diameter. The data that support this theory rest on the fact that a thin layer of iridium, an element found mainly in meteors, is present in geological strata throughout the world. (Scientists know

that the iridium itself did not cause the extinction of dinosaurs and plants, but it is simply proof that some catastrophic event involving meteors took place.)

The scientists explain that an asteroid crashed into the earth and caused huge amounts of dust and dirt to fly into the atmosphere. The dust blocked the sunlight, according to scientists, for approximately three months to a year, which caused the land to cool. Many animals died from starvation and from the cold.

One of the misunderstood things, until now, is the reason why the ocean ecology died. The ocean mass—which was then even larger than it is now—did not change temperature as drastically as did the earth. In view of the evidence, scientists have come up with an explanation. What might this explanation be?

In order to find relevant information, you might want to go through the following steps, at least mentally:

1. Restate the problem: A meteor crash killed many land animals. What information in the above description of the event might show why a meteor crash would also kill ocean animals and plants?

2. List all the information in the problem. In this problem, such information would include the following facts: (a) dinosaurs and other animals died suddenly 65 million years ago; (b) the earth was struck by a huge asteroid 10 kilometers in diameter; (c) a layer of iridium, mainly an element from meteors, is embedded throughout the earth; (d) when the meteor crashed, huge amounts of dust and dirt were thrown into the atmosphere; (e) dust blocked sunlight for three months to a year; (f) the land cooled; (g) the ocean mass was much larger than the land mass; (h) the temperature change did not affect the ocean.

3. Eliminate items of information that are probably or clearly irrelevant in solving the problem. In this case, information about the land dinosaurs and animals, the earth's being struck by the asteroid, and the layer of iridium is probably not directly relevant to this problem.

4. Consider the information that is relevant to solving the problem. In this problem, such information would include facts that might explain the results of the crash of the meteorite: it threw large amounts of dust out into the atmosphere, the dust blocked sunlight for three months to a year, the land cooled in the darkness, and the ocean temperature change was not important.

5. Think about whether or not you might be able to infer more information from the given relevant information. For example, the fact that large amounts of dust were thrown into the atmosphere would result in air pollution and blockage of sunlight. What effect might a blockage of sunlight have on the ocean ecology? What effect might pollution have on this ecology? What effect might the death of plant life in the seas, due to lack of sunlight, have upon the total food chain upon which all animals in the sea depend?

Here is another problem that provides a good example of the importance of selective encoding:

> You have black socks and blue socks in a drawer, mixed in a ratio of 4 to 5. Because it is dark, you are unable to see the colors of the socks that you take out of the drawer. How many socks do you have to take out of the drawer to be assured of having a pair of socks of the same color?

People who answer this problem incorrectly tend to focus on information in the problem that is actually irrelevant—namely, that the sock colors are mixed in a ratio of 4 to 5. There are at least three reasons why this information might *seem* to be relevant, at first reading: First, people often assume that all the quantitative information given us in a mathematical problem will be relevant to solving that problem. This assumption, however, is incorrect. Second, there is so little quantitative information in this particular problem that people would assume that each bit given would be relevant, even if they did not always make this assumption. Third, people often start to solve problems of this kind by figuring out how to use the quantitative information in the problem before they even consider whether the information is relevant to the solution of the problem. Thus, people who answer the problem incorrectly often do so because they are misled by the irrelevant information in it.

The correct answer is "three." Consider the possibilities. If the first sock is blue and the second sock is blue, you immediately have a pair; similarly, if the first sock is black and the second sock is black, you also immediately have a pair. At worst, the first sock will be blue and the second sock black, or vice versa. In this case, it will take a third sock to create a pair of one color or the other.

Another problem that requires selective encoding for its correct solution is the following:

> A teacher had 23 pupils in his class. All but 7 of them went on a museum trip and thus were away for the day. How many of them remained in class that day?

People frequently read this problem and immediately subtract 7 from 23 to obtain 16 as their answer. But this answer is incorrect. The critical word in the problem is "but." It is not the case that seven students went on the museum trip but rather that "all but 7" went on the trip. Thus, the fact that there are a total of 23 students in the class actually becomes irrelevant, even though it is one of only two numbers in the problem. The correct answer to the problem is actually the single number in the problem that is relevant to the problem's solution, namely 7.

A famous problem that is similar to the "museum"

problem and similar in its selective encoding requirements is the following:

> An airplane crashes on the U.S.–Canadian border. In what country are the survivors buried?

The correct solution to this problem requires careful reading and selective encoding of the word "survivors." Unless you read the problem very carefully, you will not come up with the correct answer that survivors are not buried. Two activities, each involving several problems that require selective encoding, are included in this book.

### Selective Combination

Consider the following problem. As you do so, think about how selective combination—putting pieces of information together in new ways—can help you solve the problem.

> There were 100 politicians at a meeting. Each politician was either honest or dishonest. We know the following two facts: First, at least 1 of the politicians was honest; second, for any 2 politicians at least 1 of the 2 was dishonest. How many of the politicians were honest and how many were dishonest, and what are the respective numbers of each?

In this particular problem, selective encoding of information is not particularly difficult. Indeed, the relevant clues—that at least 1 politician was honest and that for any 2 politicians, at least 1 was dishonest—are even emphasized. The problem is to figure out how to combine these clues.

The first clue tells you that there is at least 1 honest politician, and from this clue, you can infer that there are possibly 99 dishonest politicians. Of course, there may be fewer than 99 dishonest politicians. The second clue tells you that if you take any 2 politicians, you are guaranteed that at least 1 of them (and possibly both of them) will be dishonest. Combining these two clues gives you an answer to the problem. The second clue tells you that if you take the honest politician in the first clue and match that politician with any other of the 99 politicians, at least 1 of the 2 politicians will be dishonest. Now, since you know that the politician from the first clue is honest, it follows that the other 99 must be dishonest. There is no other way of guaranteeing that at least 1 politician in each pair will be dishonest. You can conclude, then, that there is 1 honest politician and there are 99 dishonest politicians.

Now, consider another selective combination problem that many people find to be quite difficult, despite its deceptively simple appearance.

> I bought 1 share in the Sure-Fire corporation for $70. I sold that share for $80. Eventually, I bought back the share for $90, but later sold it for $100. How much money did I make?

As in the preceding problem, the information that is relevant for solution is quite obvious. Indeed, all of the numerical information in this problem is relevant. The question is, how does one combine it? There are actually two ways to arrive at the answer. The first involves considering the two buying–selling sequences. When the share of stock is sold each time, I make a profit of $10. My total profit, therefore, is $20. Another way to solve the problem involves simply adding up the amount of money I pay in purchasing shares—$70 + $90 = $160—and subtracting that sum from the total amount of money involved in my selling of the shares—$80 + $100 = $180. The difference, again, is $20, my profit on the transactions.

### Selective Comparison

Selective-comparison problems require you to relate new information to old information. Analogies are good examples of such problems, because they require you to draw on prior knowledge. Analogies also require you to infer a relation, and then use that relation to complete a new one. However, most analogies are not particularly novel.

It is possible to create novel analogies by selectively altering states of the world. Consider the analogies below. In solving these analogies, assume that the statement given before the analogy is true, whether or not it is actually true. Then solve the analogy taking this assumption into account. Sometimes the assumption will be true in the real world; other times it will be false. Sometimes the assumption will affect the solution you reach; other times it will not. The important thing is to assume the statement is true, regardless of its actual truth or falsity, and then to use the assumption, where needed, to solve the analogies. Answers appear after the problems. In addition, we have provided an example of a novel-analogies activity that can be copied and given directly to children. As always, discussion of each item—of why, for instance, a given choice is a better solution than the others—is essential.

1. VILLAINS are lovable.
   HERO is to admiration as VILLAIN is to
   CONTEMPT   AFFECTION   CRUEL   KIND

2. CHOWDER is sour.
   CLAM is to SHELLFISH as CHOWDER is to
   SOUP   STEAK   LIQUID   SOLID

3. LAKES are dry.
   TRAIL is to HIKE as LAKE is to
   SWIM   DUST   WATER   WALK

Answers: AFFECTION, SOUP, WALK

## SUMMARY

In this goal, we have described three important kinds of insight skills: (a) selective encoding, which is used to figure out what information is relevant for a problem at hand; (b) selective combination, which is used to decide how to put together the relevant pieces of information; and (c) selective comparison, which is used to relate new information to old information. All three processes need to be developed to enhance students' insightful thinking skills, both in the classroom and in the real world. Next we examine the differences in problem solving for the everyday world versus for school thinking programs.

## GOAL 5: SELF-DIRECTED QUESTIONS AND ACTIVITIES

1 What distinguishes *special-process* views of insight from *nothing-special* views? What is the triarchic view of insight?

2 Can you think of some examples of scientific insights other than those mentioned in the text? What are they?

**3** Think of some examples of insights that you may have experienced in your work as a teacher. What are these examples?

**4** Suppose that you had the power to implement an insight-training program in your school. Would you do so? Why or why not?

**1** *Special-process* views conceptualize insight as involving processes that are qualitatively different from those involved in ordinary thinking (e.g., unconscious leaps of thought), whereas *nothing-special* views conceptualize insight as involving the same processes involved in ordinary thinking. In the triarchic view, insight involves processes (i.e., selective encoding, selective comparison, and selective combination) that are used in other kinds of thinking as well as in insightful thinking; however, in insightful thinking, these processes are applied in highly novel or unusual ways.

**2** Answers will vary, but one example involves the insight of Snow, a 19th century English physician. Snow proposed that cholera was spread through contaminated water, on the basis of the fact that those who had gotten sick in a London epidemic of cholera had used water from the same pump. Similarly, in the early 1980s, when public-health officials and scientists at the CDC saw a constellation of previously rare cancers and pneumonia in a number of young homosexual men, they had the insight that what they were looking at was an epidemic of a new, sexually transmitted disease—now known, of course, as AIDS.

**3** Answers will vary, but such insights might include insights about what motivates a particular student, insights about students' abilities, and insights about how a given student's parents influence him or her.

**4** Answers will vary.

## Goal 5: Teaching Activities

### Selective Encoding Problems (I)

*DIRECTIONS*: Decide if you have enough information to solve each problem. If information is missing, tell what is missing. If no information is missing, solve the problem.

1. Mary makes headbands and sells them for two dollars each. How much will she get for 10 headbands?

2. Roberto bought six boxes of chocolate-chip cookies at the grocery store. How many chocolate-chip cookies does he have altogether?

3. There are 10 red cars and 15 blue cars in the school parking lot. How many cars are in the parking lot?

4. On Monday, 11 children in Ms. Nelson's class had peanut-butter sandwiches for lunch. How many children in the class did not have peanut-butter sandwiches at lunch?

5. Malcolm has gained 4 pounds since his last doctor's appointment. He now weighs 58 pounds. How much did he weigh at his last appointment?

### Selective encoding problems (II)

*DIRECTIONS*: Cross out any information that is not needed to solve each problem. Underline the information that is needed. Then solve the problem.

1. There are 28 children in Mr. Davis's class. Ten of the children have dogs at home. Twelve of the children have cats at home. How many of the children in the class do not have dogs?

2. Ms. Johnson has planted three rows of tulips in her garden, with four tulips in each row. Half of the tulips are white and half are purple. How many tulips does Ms. Johnson have in her garden?

3. Jonathan went to the store to buy fruit. He bought six bananas, three apples, two plums, and a bunch of grapes. How many different kinds of fruit did Jonathan buy?

4. The Smiths want to put a fence that is 6-feet high around their property. The property is a rectangle 50 feet wide and 60 feet long. How many feet of fencing do the Smiths need to get?

5. In her kitchen cabinet, Karen has six cans of carrots, eight cans of peas, two cans of corn, and four cans of pineapple. How many cans of vegetables does she have?

## Novel Analogies

DIRECTIONS: Assume that the sentence at the beginning of each item is true. Then pick the best choice to solve the analogy.

1. ELEPHANTS are tiny.
   GNAT is to tarantula as ELEPHANT is to
   WHALE   MAMMAL   CHIPMUNK   MOSQUITO

2. WORMS are furry.
   HEDGEHOG is to prickly as WORM is to
   FUR   SLIMY   BROWN   SOFT

3. ROSES smell bad.
   COLLIE is to dog as ROSE is to
   FLOWER   GARBAGE   PERFUME   PINK

4. The SKY is green
   MOON is to pearl as SKY is to
   BLUE   EMERALD   SAPPHIRE   SILVER

5. BIRDS moo.
   CATERPILLAR is to crawl as BIRD is to
   FLY   CHIRP   COW   TREE

## Goal 5: Answer Key

**Selective Encoding Problem (I):**

1. $20.

2. Missing information: how many cookies per box.

3. Missing information: how many cars, if any, that were neither red nor blue.

4. Missing information: Total number of children in the class.

5. 54 pounds.

**Selective Encoding Problem (II):**

1. Not needed: number of children having cats. Answer to problem: 18 children.

2. Not needed: proportion of tulips of each color. Answer to the problem: 12 tulips.

3. Not needed: specific number of each fruit. Answer to the problem: four kinds of fruit.

4. Not needed: height of fence. Answer to the problem: 300 feet.

5. Not needed: information about the cans of pineapple. Answer to the problem: 16 cans.

**Novel Analogies:**

1. Whale.

2. Soft.

3. Flower.

4. Emerald.

5. Fly.

## GOAL 5: SUGGESTED READINGS

Perkins, D. N. (1981). *The mind's best work*. Cambridge, MA: Harvard University Press.

Sternberg, R. J., & Davidson, J. E. (Eds.). (1995). *The nature of insight*. Cambridge, MA: MIT Press.

Sternberg, R. J., & Lubart, T. I. (1995). *Defying the crowd: Cultivating creativity in a culture of conformity*. New York: Free Press.

# goal 6

## Understanding Basic Principles and

## Pitfalls in the Teaching of Thinking

Teaching for thinking can be enhanced if the teacher follows certain basic principles, and at the same time avoids certain common pitfalls. What are these principles and pitfalls?

# THE PRINCIPLES

Probably never before in the history of educational practice has there been a greater push to teach children to think well. The signs are everywhere: multiple alternative programs to teach thinking at a variety of ages (Covington, Crutchfield, Davies, & Olton, 1974; Feuerstein, 1980; Lipman, Sharp, & Oscanyan, 1980; Whimbey & Whimbey, 1975), tomes that review in some detail the numerous programs available (Chipman, Siegel, & Glaser, 1985; Nickerson, Perkins, & Smith, 1985), workshops for teachers and administrators sponsored by such prestigious organizations as the Association for Supervision and Curriculum Development, and an outpouring of articles on teaching critical thinking in such journals as *Educational Researcher*, *Educational Leadership*, and *Phi Delta Kappan*. It would be difficult to read anything at all in the contemporary literature of education without becoming aware of this new interest in teaching thinking.

Like other surges of interest in education (some call them fads), the present interest in teaching critical thinking is a result of a confluence of social forces. First, declining scores on tests of scholastic aptitude have called attention to the apparently declining levels of good thinking among students. Second, a number of national reports have laid at least some of the blame for our educational ills at the door of the schoolhouse, where students are somehow not learning to think as well as they should. Third, psycho-educational knowledge has reached the point at which programs for teaching critical thinking look more promising than ever before, and peddlers of such programs have not been hiding their light under a bush. Fourth, a now defunct Ministry for the Development of Intelligence in Venezuela showed that the teaching of thinking can be implemented on a massive scale with some success. Finally, there is a feeling among educators that, in trying to make students better thinkers, we have tried pretty much everything else to no avail, so that the time to teach thinking directly is surely at hand.

The history of educational reform has often seemed to

be a tale of vessels laden with lofty goals being scuttled by the means used to attain them. One of the best ways to prevent these shipwrecks is to be aware, before it is too late, of those ships that are most susceptible to sinking. Perhaps there are features of the way we teach thinking that may lead us to abandon ship prematurely. We believe that we are now running such a risk but that there is still time to do something before the ship goes down.

For the past 20 years, we have been studying thinking both as it occurs in schools and as it occurs outside them. We have been particularly interested in the nature of thinking in some of the occupations in which schoolchildren find themselves later in life. As a result of this study, we have grown increasingly disturbed by the lack of correspondence between what is required for thinking in adulthood and what is being taught in school programs intended to develop thinking. The problems of thinking in the real world do not correspond well with the problems of the large majority of programs that teach thinking. We are preparing students to deal with problems that are in many respects unlike those that they will face as adults.

Now let's discuss how the problems that people really face tend to differ from those in the thinking-based programs. Teachers need to be alert to the possibility that they will miss some of the opportunities for teaching thinking described here.

1. *In the everyday world, the first and sometimes most difficult step in problem solving is the recognition that a problem exists.* Think of Detroit. U.S. automobile makers were caught unaware when the small-car craze hit the land. Japanese automakers rushed in with a variety of small cars to suit every taste: Detroit continued to respond with large gas hogs that could put a dent in anyone's budget. The problem was not that U.S. car manufacturers had solved the small-car problem incorrectly. On the contrary, they had not even recognized that a problem existed until sales started to plummet—and by then it was too late.

Often the most important step in problem solving is recognizing that a problem exists, which is the first part of problem identification. Take some other examples. Think of the person who, after being hospitalized with a serious ailment, is told that he or she had shown a number of early signs of the disease but had never recognized them as presenting a problem of any consequence. Analogous cases may occur in business, when one employee is undermining everyone's morale, or in an individual's personal life, when the choice of a romantic partner is simply not working out. At an international level, national governments waited much too long before they recognized the scope and the urgency of the global AIDS problem. In these and similar real-life cases, training in how to solve neatly numbered and formulated problems already defined as such does not help a person recognize problems that lurk in life's dark corners. Students need help in recognizing problems, not just in solving them. Bright, critical–analytical students like Alice (see Goal 1) may be good problem solvers, but they do not always recognize the existence of problems in the first place.

Sometimes problems are invented. In creative endeavor, for example, a major distinguishing factor between more and less creative individuals—be they artists, scientists, philosophers, mathematicians, or whatever—is the size, scope, and importance of the problems they address in their work (Albert, 1983; Getzels & Jackson, 1962). Training students to solve problems already posed for them does not train them to find and select important problems on their own. We have often been impressed by how well the presenters at professional meetings have solved problems that could hardly seem less consequential. Students need to be taught not only how to solve problems, but also how to find problems that are worth solving.

2. *In everyday problem solving, it is often harder to figure out just what the problem is than to figure out how to solve it.* Having recognized the existence of a problem, it is often quite difficult to specify just what the problem is. Examples abound. A business executive might easily recognize that profits are declining but not be able to say why. A student may be receiving less than top grades in a given subject but not know what prevents him or her from getting higher grades. For years one of us received "less than top" grades on compositions and was told that his ideas were good but that his writing left something to be desired. It

was not until he was in college that someone, who was not an English teacher, told him that his sentences did not follow in a logical progression. Or think of the manufacturers and wholesalers who, in the midst of the video-game craze, produced and stocked video games as if there could never be enough. Then, when the bottom dropped out of the game market, they found themselves with an expensive and unwanted inventory. They had thought that the problem they faced was one of meeting an ever-increasing demand for their products, but instead it was one of knowing when the demand would peak. Had Richard Nixon recognized that the problem presented his administration by the Watergate affair was one of minimizing the damage of extensive disclosure rather than one of minimizing the extent of the disclosure, he might have remained in office until the end of his term. And had George Bush realized how important the economy was to the people, he very likely would have been elected to a second term.

Problems in programs that teach thinking, as well as in many other school courses, often end with a clearly worded, specific question that makes quite clear just what the problem is. We all wish that the problems of life would come to us clearly formulated. For the most part, they do not. Training in how to solve explicitly formulated problems teaches students little about how to recognize and state problems. Returning again to Alice (Goal 1), we often find good problem solvers who do not stop to think about whether they are solving the problem that truly needs to be solved.

3. *Everyday problems tend to be ill-structured.* Theorists of problem solving often distinguish between well-structured and ill-structured problems (Newell & Simon, 1972; Sternberg, 1982). Well-structured problems are those in which a set of steps leading to a solution can be explicitly and clearly laid out. Ill-structured problems are those that resist such specification of the steps to solution. On the one hand, most mathematics, physics, and chemistry problems presented in schools are well-structured problems. So are the majority of problems presented in programs for teaching thinking. On the other hand, so-called insight problems tend to be ill-structured. For example, consider

Darwin's insights that led to his theory of evolution. Clearly, no well-structured steps could be formulated to lead to such insights. Creative–synthetic thinkers like Barbara (see Goal 1) tend to be particularly good at solving ill-structured problems.

Consider such problems as how to choose the right investments, how to choose a mate, how to choose a career, or how to enjoy one's life. Any number of books exist that detail the "10 easy steps" to the solution of these vexing problems. Such books continue to be written, and the new ones continue to sell. Indeed, there will always be a market for such books precisely because none of the authors ever quite succeeds in turning these ill-structured problems into the well-structured ones that their books assure us the 10 easy steps will solve.

At some level we all know that such problems are ill-structured; yet we keep hoping that someone will discover the structure that eludes us and teach this structure for $10.95. We think that part of the reason that people are such suckers for these books is that they have been brought up on school-based problems that are conveniently well-structured. The courses people have taken (and the ones teachers may now teach) on thinking might also lead us to believe that life's problems will be well-structured. But few of life's problems are so neatly structured, and it is the solving of ill-structured rather than well-structured problems that will prepare us for the challenges we most often face.

4. *In everyday problem solving, it is not usually clear just what information will be needed to solve a given problem, nor is it always clear where the requisite information can be found.* In a typical problem in a thinking course, the information needed to solve the problem is available in the problem or is expected to be readily available in students' heads. Indeed, were the information neither in the problem nor in the head, the problem would be viewed as one requiring knowledge rather than critical thinking.

Regrettably, things are not so easy in everyday life. How does one know just what information is relevant to buying stocks? Any stockbroker who knew for sure would become very rich very fast—and not just from commissions.

Suppose you need a lawyer or a doctor fast. How do you find a good one? Where do you turn for that information? If all the information we needed to solve life's problems were readily available in the problem itself or in our heads or even in an encyclopedia, life would be very different indeed. But, perhaps unfortunately, life does not imitate thinking problems, and thinking problems certainly do not imitate life.

5. *The solutions to everyday problems depend on and interact with the contexts in which the problems are presented.* Problems in books are usually decontextualized. In one, Jack will be going to the store to buy some bread and will need to figure out how much change he will receive. In the next, Millie (no relation to Jack) will be trying to figure out how much 20 party invitations will cost. The general procedure is this: We are presented with a problem, we solve it, and we move on to another problem that has little to do with the last. Problems can be solved in isolation and without respect to the (usually minimal) context in which they appear.

Life's problems repeatedly confront us with "it depends" and other ornery qualifiers. Should you buy a house or continue renting? A realtor can tell you about the real estate market, a banker can tell you about finances, and a lawyer can tell you about establishing clear title. But what about the matter of your mother-in-law, who is ready to move in, the possibility that you will change jobs within the next year, and the question of whether you want to mow the lawn and clean the place or hire someone to do these chores? Should you change jobs or stay put? It would be nice if you could decide simply on the basis of how much you like your current job, how well you do it, and what opportunities for advancement it presents. But the answers to the questions depend on a number of things: whether you will be able to find a better job, what your wife or husband will think, how you will finance the education of your children. Unlike the problems students are taught to solve, real-world problems are deeply embedded in multiple contexts that can affect their solutions. Solving real-world problems requires a sensitivity to context. Indeed, the context is often part of the problem. Practi-cal–contextual thinkers (like Celia in Goal 1) tend to excel in practical problem solving in context, although school situations often do not let them show their strength because school problems are often so decontextualized.

6. *Everyday problems generally have no one right solution, and even the criteria for what constitutes a best solution are often not clear.* The problems students are given in school—especially in thinking courses and tests of thinking ability—usually have a "right" or "best" solution. Perhaps this is understandable in problems that involve deductive reasoning, which by definition converge on responses that are either logically correct or not. It is less understandable in the case of problems that involve inductive reasoning, which by definition have an infinite number of solutions. For example, if the number series *2, 4, 6,* appeared on a test of reasoning ability, all but the dullest adults would fill in the blank with number 8. Moreover, 8 would doubtless be the answer keyed as correct. Nevertheless, it turns out that any rational number at all is inductively correct (Skyrms, 1975).

Experimental psychologists have actually studied something called the "2, 4, 6" problem, in which individuals are asked to find the rule that the experimenter has in mind for a numerical sequence (Wason, 1960). The rule in this experiment is that the sequence is one of "increasing numbers." Individuals participating in this experiment often never discover this rule, and, if they do, it usually takes quite a bit of time. Psychologists find this surprising. But is it really so surprising given the bias of thinking problems, even inductive ones, toward a single right or best answer?

Of course, it is not only laboratory curiosities that lack single correct answers. There are no unequivocally correct solutions to most of the problems one faces in life. If such answers exist at all, they are usually obvious only through hindsight. If a wife proves to be a shrew or a husband a wife-beater, the marriage probably should not have taken place. If a company goes bankrupt, the stock probably should not have been bought. But life does not exhibit the predictability of a thinking problem, and much of what we have to learn about solving problems in real life is how to deal with unpredictable and poorly predictable consequences.

7. *The solutions of everyday problems depend at least as much on informal as on formal knowledge.* In a study of how college teachers and business executives think, we asked successful individuals in each of these fields to tell us what they needed to know in order to succeed on the job (Sternberg & Wagner, 1993; Wagner & Sternberg, 1985, 1986). With stunning regularity, our subjects told us that the formal knowledge that they had learned in school had little to do with their success. Rather, they relied primarily on informal knowledge in their thought and action. Such knowledge was acquired on the job, essentially through osmosis: It was never explicitly taught and may never have been verbalized. For this reason, we have sometimes referred to such knowledge as *tacit*.

For business executives, examples of informal knowledge include knowledge of the kinds of behavior that are valued in the company for which they work—or the kinds of tasks that command high priority in their jobs—and of the kinds of products that are likely to sell. For college teachers, examples of such knowledge include ways to control activity in a classroom, how to convey material in a way that will be meaningful to the largest number of students, and how to keep students interested. All these things could, in principle, be taught, but it seems to be only through experience that they are really learned.

Some good examples of tacit knowledge needed by elementary and secondary teachers include behavior management (e.g., dealing with various kinds of misbehavior, and setting up one's classroom so as to help prevent behavior problems in the first place); dealing with parents (e.g., conducting routine parent–teacher conferences, recruiting parent volunteers for the classroom, working with parents when a child is having a serious problem or needs special education); grading (e.g., making up tests, filling out report cards, evaluating students' work on an everyday basis); scheduling (e.g., scheduling around the needs of students who have to leave the classroom for special education, speech, etc.); and managing ancillary responsibilities such as bus duty, cafeteria duty, and so forth.

Of course, in order to do well in school, children also must acquire tacit knowledge. Some examples of tacit knowledge needed by children include knowing how to get along with teachers and with other students, how to manage one's time to get assignments done, how to study for exams, and how to take notes. Debbie, whose story we discussed at the beginning of this book, was able to function well in the regular classroom despite weak analytical abilities because she had excellent tacit knowledge. It is very useful to make tacit knowledge explicit to children through open discussion. Toward this end, we have provided an example of a tacit-knowledge activity that can be used with middle-school or secondary-level students.

One might jump to the conclusion that the ability to acquire informal knowledge is simply one more manifestation of the ability to acquire *any* knowledge. Indeed, one might expect levels of informal knowledge to be highly correlated with IQ, which is in large part determined by critical-thinking skills. But our research indicates that, to the contrary, the level of informal knowledge is only weakly correlated with IQ and, in many cases, the correlations are not even statistically significant (as exemplified by Debbie's story). Moreover, level of informal knowledge predicts job success, so that it is likely that the thinking that individuals are doing on their jobs draws on skills that are unlike the critical-thinking skills that we so readily—and so easily—measure.

8. *Solutions to important everyday problems have consequences that matter*. If a student is enrolled in a course, be it thinking or something else, the consequences of solving a problem incorrectly are usually trivial. Even if the student solves large numbers of problems incorrectly, the worst consequence will probably be a lower grade in just one of many courses taken throughout the student's lifetime. The same cannot be said for real-life problems. The trivial ones, of course, may have trivial consequences, perhaps even less important than a low grade. But the important problems may have consequences as profound as

life and death—or a life of happiness versus a life of misery. If the solutions to life's problems could be separated from their consequences, then there would be no reason to worry about the way problem solving is taught in typical courses on thinking. But solutions cannot be separated from consequences, because the solution usually depends to some extent on the possible consequences of alternative solutions.

Consider elective surgery, for example. One of the authors' aunts once seriously considered an elective surgical procedure that might have relieved a source of pain she was experiencing at the time. When she was asked to sign a statement of informed consent that listed all possible negative repercussions of the surgery (including an all-too-rapid demise), she changed her mind. Or consider any major life decisions such as getting married or divorced, choosing a career, or buying a house. Such decisions cannot be made without considering the possible consequences, and the consequences may end up changing the decision one ultimately makes. Solving inconsequential problems does little to teach students to solve the consequential problems of life.

9. *Everyday problem solving often occurs in groups.* Faculty members at colleges and universities are often chosen largely on the basis of their individual problem-solving skills. All the faculty members at our own institutions, for example, have demonstrated their ability to solve significant problems in their chosen field. Yet we have often been appalled at what happens when these very individuals get together in a group such as a faculty committee meeting. The same individuals who have demonstrated beyond a doubt their skill in solving problems individually seem to be at an utter loss when they approach a problem in a group.

Many everyday problems are not usually—indeed cannot be—solved individually. At work, committees, task forces, and consortia of various kinds are regularly formed to solve problems. At home, certain decisions require input from the entire family and rightfully require a group decision-making process. But groups are susceptible to a large variety of biases in problem solving and decision making, and solving problems individually does not prepare one to deal with these sources of bias. For example, Irving Janis documented how respected government leaders, all of whom had shown themselves to be excellent individual decision makers, got into political fiascoes when put into groups (Janis, 1972). They became victims of "groupthink" and, as a group, failed to display the same powers of problem solving and decision making that they had as individuals. They had been taught to think at some of the finest institutions of higher learning in the country—but they had been taught to think only as individuals, not as members of a group.

10. *Everyday problems can be complicated, messy, and stubbornly persistent.* Even the most complicated of problems in courses on thinking are simple compared with some of the problems one has to face in everyday life. Moreover, these textbook problems tend to be much neater than the ones people confront when they leave school. But the nicest part of the problems encountered in textbooks is that, for the most part, they go away when one leaves school. Life's problems generally do not. They are there when we want them to be, but they are still there when we don't. They intrude on us and sometimes consume us, and sometimes we need skills for putting them aside and moving on to other things, lest we be paralyzed by our inability either to solve a given problem or to move on to another.

To make matters worse, problems often do not go away even after they are solved. In the work of business executives we studied, for example, and in our own work as well, solving a problem is one thing, but convincing people of the rightness of one's solution is another. Our participants too often found that all their problem solving was for naught, because they were unable to persuade the right people of the feasibility or desirability of their solutions. In these cases, the problem did not end with its solution: rather, it had just begun.

The problem of teaching thinking does not end either with the implementation of the above principles. Rather, it too has just begun. We need to take into account not only these principles but also some pitfalls.

## THE PITFALLS

In solving problems, there are usually more ways to fail than to succeed. The problem of teaching thinking is no exception. If we think of the problems that arise in teaching thinking, we usually think of the problems that confront us once we actually embark on our expedition. But in talking about the teaching of thinking to audiences of teachers and administrators, we have come to the conclusion that many programs are doomed to failure before they even begin. When these programs fail, it is not because of what is done in the classroom, but because of what is done before the program ever reaches the classroom. Some of our ideas about teaching and learning—no matter how well they may apply in the normal course of classroom events—do not apply in the case of instruction in thinking.

The following eight fallacies obstruct the teaching of thinking before we even begin and make it easy to fail. The effects of these fallacies on the teaching of thinking are both insidious and pernicious (Sternberg, 1987b).

1. *The teacher is the teacher and the student is the learner.* Normally, we teachers think of ourselves and our peers as the teachers, and we think of our students as the learners. In the typical course of teaching, this is true. We are expert in biology or English or history or whatever, and we attempt to convey some of our expertise to our students. We would feel rather guilty teaching a course in which we were not expert. Indeed, we would probably feel like fakers or cheaters.

But this common assumption does not hold in the domain of thinking. All of us—teachers and students alike—have a long way to go before we become masters of thinking. The authors have lectured about thinking to teachers and administrators on the one hand, and to high school and college students on the other. In the course of delivering these lectures, we have asked our audiences to solve some thinking problems along with us. To put it bluntly, the teachers and administrators are no better than the students. Sometimes they are worse.

It is interesting to speculate on why the teachers are

sometimes worse than the students. Is it because they are poorer thinkers or less intelligent? We strongly doubt it. Rather, they often lack the openness and receptivity of the students. They are less willing to shake free of the traces of their own expertise. Consider an example.

One of us was presenting a fairly difficult logico-mathematical problem to a mid-sized audience of teachers and administrators. As usual, he asked the audience to vote on the correct answer, and as usual, the large majority answered the problem incorrectly. This outcome is common with this particular problem. A mathematics teacher in the audience, however, answered it correctly. That is, he had the right intuitions about why an outcome that would not seem to be a logical certainty was, in fact, a logical certainty. The author asked him to explain to the audience how he arrived at his answer. Instead of tracking his intuitions, which were good, he attempted to find a mathematical theorem that would guarantee the correctness of his answer, and he ended up confusing both himself and the audience.

The interesting feature of this interaction was that the mathematics teacher's intuitions were good but he would not allow them free rein. He felt obliged to justify them in the ordinary currency of his subject. In other words, his expertise impeded his critical-thinking processes. Too often, expertise, when we let it "take us over," impairs rather than facilitates our thinking. Quite simply, we teachers must look at ourselves, as well as our students, as learners, and we must become comfortable in this role. In our first year or two of teaching, we know that we have almost as much to learn as the students, but we rarely acknowledge this fact. In teaching critical thinking, we must acknowledge our own need for development and create an atmosphere in the classroom that allows us to be comfortable with this fact. Moreover, we must not feel threatened by this somewhat unusual role. There is no better way to learn than to teach, and both we and our students must accept ourselves in our dual role as learner and teacher.

2. *Thinking is the students' job and only the students' job.* This fallacy is related to the first one and places the burden of thinking on the student, not the teacher. One can

see the fallacy at work in the classrooms of teachers who wait for students to think out responses, but who clearly are not thinking out responses themselves. This insidious attitude is at work even before the teacher enters the classroom.

One of us once presented to the upper level administrators in a local school district an hour-long lecture on principles of choosing programs for teaching thinking. His goal was to enable these administrators to choose programs intelligently. During the questions that followed the lecture, he should have expected the inevitable question: "All of this is nice," one administrator said, "but let's get down to nuts and bolts. Which program should we use?" She wanted to be told. The last thing she wanted was to think about which program would be right for her district, given the mix of children, resources, teachers, and so on. Thinking, like charity, has to start at home—in this case, with those who plan to teach.

We have seen similar responses when we have been asked about teacher training. Some teachers want to adapt a given program or set of program ideas to their own school contexts. But other teachers want to be told exactly what to do. They are literally afraid to add anything of their own or to think about how they might implement a program in a way that would best meet their own needs and those of their students. Yet they must not be afraid to do what they are asking their students to do.

Program developers and salespeople—often the same individuals—sometimes discourage in their prospective customers the very skills that their programs are supposed to develop in children. They present a smooth, slick sales pitch that rivals the best cigarette and alcohol advertising in its ability to quench the critical capacities of its intended audience. Moreover, they will often have little or nothing good to say about any program other than their own. Teachers must evaluate programs presented for classroom use in the same way that they want their students to evaluate problems presented to them in the programs.

3. *The most important thing is to decide on the correct program.* We mentioned above that we are often asked to share which thinking-based program is best. Well, *no* program

is best. First, assuming a school or district does not opt to create a program of its own, the choice of a program must be tailored to specific students, teachers, resources, and the like. But, most important, a program must be tailored to the goals of the users. Many teachers and administrators who are eager to adopt thinking-based programs have given only minimal thought to what their goals are in selecting (or designing) such a program. Yet the various programs—almost all of which promise to promote thinking, intellectual skills, or something similar—often address quite different things. Some concentrate almost exclusively on analytic problem solving, and virtually all the problems are mathematical and logical, with single correct answers. Is that the kind of thinking we wish to develop? Other programs make use of problems that are practically indistinguishable from those on conventional intelligence tests. Do we primarily wish to improve scores on IQ tests? Still other programs attempt to develop creative or synthetic thinking skills, but they do not emphasize critical or analytic thinking skills—not even evaluation of the products of creative thinking. Do we wish to develop creative thinking alone, without critical thinking to accompany it?

Our point is a simple one. If teachers and administrators have a very clear sense of their goals in implementing a thinking-skills program, the choice of a program will become fairly straightforward. But they must decide on their goals *before* they decide on a program. They should not let the choice of the program decide what they wish to accomplish. For many years, the problems that happened to appear on intelligence tests limited thinking about intelligence. Let's not let the same thing happen with training in thinking. First, decide on goals, and only then decide on how to go about accomplishing them.

In addition, the choice of a program involves a complex set of other, apparently binary choices, such as infused versus separate instruction or process-based versus holistic instruction. In infused instruction, for instance, thinking skills are taught as a part of the regular curriculum, infused into a variety of context areas, whereas in separate instruction, thinking skills are taught as a separate subject. Similarly, teaching thinking programs can involve teaching component thinking processes individually, or can emphasize a more holistic approach to thinking instruction.

Have you ever noticed, however, that very few really important choices are truly binary? Decisions almost always involve more than two options, and sometimes a mixture of options is best. For example, a problem posed as a binary choice between going to graduate school full-time or not going at all may lead someone to decide that there just is no time, money, or whatever to make it through. But if you consider the many ways to obtain a graduate degree (short of simply buying one), it turns out that the decision is much more complex than it initially seemed.

We have taken part in any number of pointless debates about whether critical-thinking instruction should be infused or separate, whether it should be holistic or process-based, whether it should be analytic or synthetic, and so on. The debates are pointless because the answer is almost always "some combination of both." Yet these debates could leave the impression that "both" is an unacceptable answer. We can force ourselves into making decisions that should never have been made in the first place.

Many good reasons have been adduced for both separate and for infused instruction. For example, separate instruction insures that there will be a time and a place for teaching thinking skills, helps prevent the instruction from being watered down, and makes it easier to see how the principles of critical thinking fit together. Infused instruction facilitates transfer to a variety of situations, shows that critical thinking should be part and parcel of all thinking, and is more practical in many instructional settings. But often it is better to strive for some meaningful combination of both separate and infused instruction. It is important for students to learn component skills, but they must also learn to see how these skills fit into a whole. In addition, students need to learn to think both analytically and synthetically.

Artificial dichotomies impede rather than facilitate efforts to develop critical thinking in children and in ourselves. If presented with a supposedly dichotomous choice about teaching thinking, ask first whether the choice is truly dichotomous. Might there be a third option that is better than the two that are presented, especially one that allows the best of both worlds? Remember that artificial dichotomies are common in education: whole-language versus code-emphasis in reading, discovery learning versus direct instruction, individual versus cooperative learning, and so on.

5. *What really counts is the right answer.* The bottom line in all multiple choice, short-answer, and similar tests is the correct answer. It really does not matter how a student arrives at that answer. Most tests of thinking are short-answer or multiple-choice tests, so the same principle that applies to typical ability and achievement tests also applies to them. Of course, short-answer and multiple-choice formats expedite convenient mass testing. But they also instill a frame of mind that is unfortunate if carried over to the teaching of thinking.

In one of our presentations on teaching thinking, we posed a difficult mathematical insight problem that could be answered yes or no. Although in such problems half of the people who respond can answer correctly by chance alone, actually only a small fraction of a typical audience knows *why* the correct answer is correct. A superintendent in the audience raised his hand and answered the question correctly. When he was asked to justify his answer, it became clear that he had followed a convoluted course of reasoning that had nothing to do with the problem. Told (by other members of the audience) that his reasoning left something to be desired, he was flabbergasted. And it became clear that he could not care less. After all, he had answered the question correctly. What more was necessary?

It is difficult to balance a process orientation toward solving problems with a product orientation. Most teachers are so used to scoring products that they often have trouble taking processes seriously. We have seen teachers of thinking who will follow the logical chains that lead to correct answers, but who clearly share the superintendent's view: They want right answers. But very often in thinking-based problems, there are no right answers. And even when there are, it is the thought process that counts. Ultimately, students who think well will be in a position to generate good answers, whereas students who generate good answers do not always think well.

6. *Class discussion is primarily a means to an end.* We teachers tend to think about class discussion in the same way that we think about the processes of thinking. That is, we consider processes as means to an end. But in teaching thinking, the processes of thought and their expression in class discussion are legitimate and important ends in their own right. Traditionally, psychologists conceived of thought as something that originates inside the individual, and only then is expressed socially. Psychologists have recently come to realize the great extent to which thought emerges as a social process and is internalized only after it has been socially expressed. Have you ever noticed how hard it is for members of a group to pin down who first had which ideas? Isn't it frustrating to work with people in a group who must always get credit for every idea they *think* they have come up with?

One of us spent an entire day in a meeting at a group-oriented company. The author was astonished by the success of the meeting. More good ideas came out in that one day than the author had ever seen come out of any meeting in more than a decade. The author started reflecting on why this was so and concluded that it was because no one cared about who had which ideas. The goal was to produce the very best possible collective product.

In our meetings at universities, however, this healthy group mentality had not been allowed to emerge. People were very concerned about ownership of ideas and with promoting their own ideas. Compromise was seen as capitulation, and in exchange for such giving-in one would expect to receive something in return. As a result, the quality of the meetings was never what it might have been.

Because collective effort is so important in daily life and because psychologists now realize that at least a substantial portion of one's ability to think originates outside oneself, teachers must view class discussion as more than just a peripheral part of a thinking-skills program. Discussion is essential. In our society, we tend to value most those individual efforts that yield a concrete, written product. This value system does not provide the best or most comprehensive approach to the teaching of thinking skills.

7. *Mastery-learning principles can be applied to learning to think, just as they can be applied to anything else.* A while ago, one of us spoke to a large meeting of a state affiliate of the Association for Supervision and Curriculum Development. He was asked how to apply principles of testing for mastery learning to thinking skills programs, regardless of the program in question. The easy answer: You can't. Mastery learning may or may not apply in other domains, but it does not apply to the learning of thinking. What does the concept of 80% or 90% "correct" really mean on a test of thinking? Not much, because one can obtain whatever set of scores one wishes by varying the difficulty of the test, or broadening the range of answers considered correct. It is best to think of thinking as developing depth in successive layers, without any limit to the possible depth one can achieve.

Consider, for example, a problem one of us uses in his own text, a problem regarding disarmament (Sternberg, 1986). Students are asked to think of ways to initiate and carry out a set of negotiations leading to mutual disarmament. There is no right or wrong answer. Percentage values mean nothing. When students are given this problem near the beginning of the course, they tend to see only its surfaces, and they offer fairly trivial solutions to this extremely complex problem. After having been in the course for a while, they see much more depth in the problem, and consequently they provide much more depth in their solutions. Similarly, most of the activities and questions that accompany this book do not have a single "right" answer, but rather can involve a range of good responses that vary in their complexity and depth.

Like most other real-world problems, this one has no clearly defined right or wrong answer. What students learn from a good course on thinking is how to approach deep and complex problems in deep and complex ways. Poor problem solvers may become good ones; good ones may become excellent ones. But the concept of mastery does not apply, because there is no "ceiling" to the level of performance.

This fact has implications for the question of who should receive instruction in thinking. The answer: everyone. No matter how well they think, everyone can stand improvement, and everyone can improve. Certainly there may be genetically determined limits to how well a particular child may eventually be able to think. But let's worry about those limits when we reach them—and so far we haven't.

8. *The job of a course in thinking is to teach thinking.* This fallacy sounds so plausible that it is hard to believe that it is fallacious. Yet it is. Students may ultimately learn to think, but not because we taught them. In a very real sense, they must teach themselves, and all teachers can do is provide every possible means to enable this self-instruction to take place. There is nothing more pathetic than a teacher who tries to *teach* a student to think for him or herself. We have seen it many times. The teacher tells the student what the problem is, how to pose the problem, the way (rarely ways) to solve the problem, and then leaves it to the student to do the "problem solving." If the student then solves the problem correctly, both the teacher and the student believe that instruction in critical thinking has occurred. And perhaps it has, but only in the most trivial and impoverished ways. The teacher has done the most important thinking for the student and has left the student with only the most routine aspects of problem solving to complete. The teacher will probably be surprised later, when the skill that was supposedly learned does not transfer to other situations.

It has often been said that there is no better way to learn than to teach. If this is so, then teachers must let students teach themselves to a large extent. Teachers need to serve not strictly as teachers, but as facilitators, and they must simultaneously recognize that they, too, are learners. Teachers must also recognize that individual differences abound in the learning strategies of their students, so that what works for one student may not work for another. Hence, students must ultimately teach themselves, for they must be responsible for finding out what methods of problem finding and problem solving work for them.

## SUMMARY

In this section, we have discussed some principles and pitfalls in the teaching of thinking. Keeping these ideas in mind can greatly enhance the teaching of thinking. For example, every one of the eight fallacies we have discussed above can be avoided and replaced with a more useful and more effective strategy. Instruction in thinking skills is both possible and desirable, but it is not simple, and we teachers need to do all that we can to make it work. Above all, we must guard against assumptions that undermine our efforts before we have even begun. One of these assumptions is that teaching children to be good thinkers is solely a matter of teaching cognitive thought processes. If children fail to think well, the origins are often not cognitive at all, as shown in the discussion of the final goal.

**1** Select a textbook or curriculum guide that you use regularly (e.g., in mathematics, science, or social studies) and analyze some of the problems contained in it. Do these problems tend to exemplify the kinds of "school" problems discussed in this section? If so, how? If not, how not?

**2** Think of a specific "everyday" problem in your life as a teacher (e.g., scheduling, classroom management, dealing with parents). Contrast the characteristics of this problem with the kinds of academic problems that students tend to solve in school.

**3** Develop some everyday problems that would be especially appropriate for your own students. Then, if possible, actually try out the problems with your class.

**1** Answers will vary, but "school" problems tend, among other things, to be well-defined and well-structured; to be presented in a decontextualized manner; to have one right answer; to depend on academic (i.e., formal) knowledge; and to be solved by individuals rather than by people working in groups.

**2** Answers will vary, but everyday problems tend to be

- difficult to define

- ill-structured

- highly dependent on context

- dependent on tacit (i.e., informal) knowledge as well as on formal knowledge

- complicated and persistent

- solved in groups

- characterized by more than one possible answer

- accompanied by consequences that matter

**3** Answers will vary.

## Goal 6: Teaching Activities

### Tacit Knowledge Activity

*DIRECTIONS*: Tacit knowledge is knowledge that is usually learned from experience rather than taught directly in school. In the scenarios below, each student is having trouble in school not because of lack of ability or lack of motivation, but because of a lack of tacit knowledge about certain skills that are important to school success. For each scenario, specify the tacit knowledge that the students are lacking and how they might begin to remedy their problem.

1. Marcus rarely does well on exams, even though he studies hard and actually knows most of the material well. For one thing, he always seems to emphasize the wrong material in studying. For example, his last history exam was on the American Revolution and Marcus memorized the names, dates, and locations of all the major battles of the war. However, none of this information was tested on the exam. In addition, Marcus sometimes loses credit for failing to answer questions. On the history test, he spent most of his time answering the multiple-choice part of the test, on which he did fairly well. However, he lost a lot of credit because he didn't have time to answer two of the three essay questions on the test.

2. Tiffany's grades are suffering because she often does not hand in homework. Tiffany's teachers think that Tiffany is just lazy, but in fact, Tiffany spends several hours each night doing homework. However, she is overwhelmed by the amount of work she has to do and cannot get everything completed. Last week she spent hours on a project that is due in biology next month, but she didn't manage to get any of her daily Spanish assignments done. Even when she does get assignments completed, she often loses them or forgets to bring them to school.

3. Steven's math class emphasizes cooperative group activities. At first, many of the other students wanted to work with Steven, who is an excellent student with a particular aptitude for mathematics. However, things are not going well in Steven's group. Steven can't understand what's wrong, because he knows he is good in math and he is even willing to do the lion's share of the work. Yesterday, one of the other students in the group exploded at Steven, saying, "Shut up! I'm sick of you always putting down my ideas!" None of the other students came to Steven's defense.

## Goal 6: Answer Key

### Tacit Knowledge Activity

1. Examples of tacit knowledge needed by Marcus: how to study for exams (e.g., talk to teachers or to other students about which material will be emphasized in testing); how to take tests (e.g., budget time so that he will be able to complete the entire test).

2. Examples of tacit knowledge needed by Tiffany: how to prioritize tasks (e.g., if the biology project is not due for a month, she doesn't have to get all of it done in one week); organizational skills (e.g., put homework in a place where she will see it and will not forget to bring it to school).

3. Examples of tacit knowledge needed by Steven: how to get along with other students (e.g., listen to others' ideas, share control of tasks with others).

## GOAL 6: SUGGESTED READINGS

Feuerstein, R. (1979). *The dynamic assessment of retarded performers: The learning potential assessment device, theory, instruments, and techniques.* Baltimore, MD: University Park Press.

Sternberg, R. J., Okagaki, L., & Jackson, A. (1990). Practical intelligence for success in school. *Educational Leadership, 48*, 35–39.

Williams, W. M., Blythe, T., White, N., Li, J., Sternberg, R. J., & Gardner, H. I. (1996). *Practical intelligence for school: A handbook for teachers of grades 5–8*. New York: Harper-Collins.

# goal 7

## Understanding Why Good
## Thinkers Fail (Too Often)

Everyone fails sometimes. Indeed, it is doubtful that we could ever learn if we never failed at anything. The sign of good thinking is not never making mistakes, but rather learning from those mistakes so that they are not made again and again. A good thinker can be forgiven for making mistakes, but perhaps not for making the same mistakes repeatedly.

Almost all of us know seemingly good thinkers who make mistakes too often and who fail at what they do too often. It is as though their good thinking is for naught when they confront problems of the real world. Clearly, good thinking is not enough for successful performance in the everyday world, no matter how broadly good thinking is defined. People can come into the world with some of the best intellectual gifts heredity has to offer, or they can be brought up in a highly advanced environment, or they can read a book such as this and practice their intellectual skill, and they can still routinely make a mess of their lives. Unless they can circumvent or otherwise bypass the stumbling blocks that get in the way of optimal intellectual performance, they may find that most, if not all, of their intellectual gifts are of little value. Conversely, highly accomplished people generally succeed not only because of their natural talents, but also because of other personal qualities, an idea illustrated by our final activity ("Why Good Thinkers Succeed").

The discussion of this goal presents 20 stumbling blocks that can get in the way of even the best thinkers (Sternberg, 1986). For the most part, these stumbling blocks are not strictly intellectual ones, but if people can keep these sorts of problems under control, then they can truly concentrate upon developing their intellects, knowing that this development will reflect itself in improved task performance. As you read the 20 impediments to the full realization of good thinking, it may become increasingly obvious to you why conventional intelligence tests, and perhaps even more broadly defined ones, can account for only a relatively small proportion of variance in real-world performance.

1. *Lack of Motivation.* It scarcely matters what talents people have if they are not motivated to use them. In many if not most environments, motivation counts at least as much as intellectual skills in the attainment of success. The reason motivation is so important is that individuals within a given environment—for example, a classroom—tend to represent a relatively narrow range of ability, but a much broader range of motivation. Motivation thus becomes a key source of individual differences in success. For some

people, motivation will come from external sources—approval of peers, attainment of recognition, attainment of money, or whatever. For others, motivation will be internal, deriving from their own satisfaction in a job well-done. Most people will be both internally and externally motivated in different proportions. Whatever the source of motivation, it is critical to the expression of intelligence and to success.

On the whole, it is probably preferable for motivation to be internally rather than externally generated for the reason that external sources of motivations tend to be transient. As a result, people who are primarily externally motivated are likely to lose their motivation if the external sources of reward diminish or disappear. Internally motivated individuals are able to maintain their motivation over the rises and falls of external rewards. For instance, children who are motivated primarily by stars, stickers, or other tangible rewards often lose their motivation when the rewards are unavailable, whereas children who have an intrinsic interest in a topic have a natural motivation for learning that is more easily sustained.

2. *Lack of impulse control.* There are times in life when people need to act impulsively, but impulsive behavior tends to detract from rather than enhance intellectual work. Teachers sometimes encounter children who are capable of doing excellent academic work, but whose capabilities are largely unrealized due to the children's tendency to work impulsively and without reflection. In one of his earliest books, L. L. Thurstone (1924) claimed that a key feature of intelligent persons is their ability to control impulsive responses. Many years later a comparative psychologist, D. Stenhouse (1973), independently came to the same conclusion. Habitual impulsiveness gets in the way of optimal intellectual performance by not allowing people to bring their full intellectual resources to bear on a problem. Although endless reflection is also clearly undesirable, people should not let themselves get carried away by the first solution that occurs to them in attempting to solve a problem. Better solutions may arise after further thought.

3. *Lack of perseverance and perseveration.* Some people,

despite all their intelligence, give up too easily. If things do not immediately go their way, or if their initial attempts at something are unsuccessful, they drop whatever they are doing. They thereby lose the opportunity to complete, possibly in a highly suitable way, the tasks they undertake. It is as though the least frustration of any kind is enough to keep them from persevering. At the other extreme are people who continue working on a problem long after they should have quit. They perseverate even after it should have become clear to them that they are going to be unable to solve the problem, at least at that time. Alternatively, they may basically have solved the problem, but they then go on to solve it again and again. One can see in certain scholarly careers the existence of this tendency toward perseveration. The scholar conducts an important piece of work, perhaps as his or her PhD thesis, then follows up the work with some subsequent studies that address what are usually the more minor problems that evolve out of that initial work. At some point, people in the field generally expect that scholar to move on to another problem, or at least to a different approach to the same problem. Instead, the scholar continues to do what to most people appears to be the same research, over and over again. There may be minor changes in or additions to the research, but from the point of view of practically anyone but the scholar, the scholarly contribution essentially ceased long ago. Perseveration occurs in other areas of life as well. Almost everyone knows someone who, having been rejected repeatedly by a potential romantic partner, nevertheless keeps trying again and again, despite the persistence of negative signals from the potential partner. It is as though the person is unable to stop in a fruitless quest. He or she perseverates long after it has become obvious to everyone else, and sometimes even to the person, that he or she is making no headway.

4. *Using the wrong abilities.* Many people become aware, at some time during their lives, that they are either in the wrong occupation, or that they are going about the occupation they are in incorrectly. It is as though the work they are doing requires one set of abilities, and they are attempting to do it with a different set of abilities. This phe-

nomenon, of course, can occur during their schooling as well as in later life. They may find themselves in law school and realize that their cognitive abilities would have been better suited to an academic career. Or they may find themselves in medical school and come to the conclusion that their real abilities lie in sales. Or they may find that they are brilliant in their area of expertise, but poor in the teaching of that area of expertise. Their discovery, basically, is that they do have strong abilities, but not for the kind of tasks in which they are engaged. At such points, the intelligent thing to do may be to select another course of schooling or career, or at least switch study or career strategies. Sometimes, we find that the critical–analytical "Alices" (see Goal 1), who are so strong in their school performance, do not excel equally once they are actually on the job rather than in school preparing for their job.

5. *Inability to translate thought into action*. Some people are very adept at coming up with solutions to their problems, and may actually seem to have a solution for everything in their lives as well as in the lives of other people, but they seem unable to translate their thought into action. In the words of the psychologist E. R Guthrie (1935), they become "buried in thought." No matter how good their ideas, they rarely seem to be able to do anything about them. In order to capitalize fully on intelligence, one must have not only good ideas, but the ability to do something about these ideas—to translate thought into action. Almost everyone knows of people who have made an important decision for their lives, but seem unable to act on it. Having decided to get married, for example, they cannot set a date. When it comes to action, paralysis sets in. Whatever their level of intelligence, such people are unable to benefit from it. At times, we are all like this. The problem we face is to do something about it and to act when appropriate rather than remaining buried in thought.

6. *Lack of product orientation*. Some people seem very concerned about the process by which things are done, but not nearly as concerned about the resulting product. Yet it is primarily on the basis of what one produces that one's accomplishments are judged, whether in school or in later life. We have had students who have done really classy re-

search, but when it comes to writing up their research, they do a clearly second- or third-rate job. They were very involved in the process of the research, but they lost their involvement and enthusiasm once it was time to turn that process into a final product. As a result, their contributions are not seen as being as important as they potentially could be, and their full level of intelligence does not manifest itself. One sees a similar type of problem with some children, who have very creative, interesting ideas, and may do well in writing initial drafts of composition, but fall short when it comes to polishing the final product.

7. *Inability to complete tasks and to follow through.* The one certain prediction about "noncompleters" is that whatever they begin they will not finish. Nothing in their lives ever seems to draw quite to a close. Perhaps they are afraid to finish things for fear that they will not know what to do with themselves next. Or they may overwhelm themselves with the details of a project, becoming so hopelessly enmeshed that they are unable to progress. The lives of these people often seem to embody Zeno's paradox. In this paradox, a man wishes to get from point A to point B. In order to traverse the distance, he has to traverse half the distance. In order to traverse the remaining half of the distance, he has first to traverse half of that distance, leaving one quarter of the total distance remaining to be traversed. But in order to traverse that distance, he first has to do half of that. In the paradox, the man always goes half the remaining distance without ever arriving. Similarly, in the situations life presents, some people seem unable to reach the end.

8. *Failure to initiate.* Other people seem unwilling or unable to initiate projects; they are always trying to decide what to do. Often, this inability to initiate results from fear of commitment. These people are afraid to become too committed to anything, and as a result they are unwilling to undertake anything. Consider, for example, the problem of a student trying to decide on a dissertation topic. Some students fail to complete graduate school because they can never commit themselves to a topic. A dissertation requires a substantial investment of time and energy, and some students are simply unwilling to make this com-

mitment. Many people act this way in interpersonal relationships. They never seem to want to go beyond just meeting other people, for fear of becoming committed to the relationship. As a result, they go through life in a series of superficial relationships, unable to initiate anything more substantial that runs the risk of leading to a commitment.

9. *Fear of failure*. Fear of failure seems to start early in life. This problem is very common, especially in individuals at the extremes of the continuum in achievement. Perhaps low achievers fear failure because they have experienced too much of it; perhaps for high achievers, the problem is that they have not learned to accept occasional failures as a normal part of learning. To some extent, one of us can see it at work in his own son. He is very able, but sometimes seems unwilling to undertake things for fear of failing at them. Many people fail to realize their full intellectual potential because of their fear that they will fail at what they do. In college, they may not take the difficult courses that they need because they do not expect to do well in them. As a result, they may do well in the courses they take, but later have no use for those courses. Later on, as lawyers or doctors or scientists or business executives, they may not undertake the projects that could really make a difference to their careers because of their fear that the projects will not succeed. Indeed, they may not even enter the occupation of their choice because of their fear that they will not succeed in it, or they may not continue with a personal relationship, not because of the way it is going, but because of their fear of the way it might go.

In some cases, fear of failure may be realistic. If the consequences of failure are high enough, fear of failure can be quite adaptive. For example, the whole strategy of nuclear deterrence depends on fear of failure—the theory being that no country will start a nuclear war because of the fear that it will be a disaster for them as well as for their opponents. Thus, there are times at which it is quite reasonable not to take risks. But there are other times when one must take risks, and the unwillingness or inability to do so results in loss of life opportunities that may never return.

10. *Procrastination*. Procrastination seems to be a uni-

versal fact of life. Everyone, at some time or another, procrastinates, putting off for later the things they know should be done now. Procrastination becomes a serious problem only when it is a uniform strategy in one's way of doing things. Some graduate students tend always to be looking for little things to do so as to put off the big things. They always manage to get their daily reading and assignments done, but seem to procrastinate forever in undertaking the large-scale projects that can really make a difference to their careers. Similarly, some younger students do well in day-to-day classroom work, but procrastinate when it comes to studying for exams or writing papers, and so end up with grades that do not reflect their actual abilities. In any career or stage of life, it is easy to become immersed in the daily trivia that can gobble up all of one's time. The tendency to become so immersed may actually result in short-term success, but often results in long-term failure. Those with a tendency toward procrastination often have to force themselves to undertake the big things, because they are simply unable to do them without pressure, whether self-imposed or imposed from the outside.

11. *Misattribution of blame.* Some people feel they can do no wrong, and are always looking for others to blame for even the slightest mishap. Others are always blaming themselves for everything, regardless of their role in the event or events that led to mishap. Misattribution of blame can seriously hinder one's intellectual self-realization. For example, one of us had a graduate student working with him who was very able and competent in research. The faculty thought the world of her, and yet she always blamed herself for anything that went wrong. It reached the point where she felt that she could do nothing right, and she seemed traumatized much of the time. Eventually, she left our program. Another graduate student was exactly the opposite. She always managed to blame others for things that went wrong in her graduate career. Although it was clear to practically everyone surrounding her that she was just not working very hard, she always had an excuse for why things were not getting done, and the excuse tended to involve the machinations of others that prevented her from

working and reaching her goals. Misattributions of blame close the door to self-improvement.

12. *Excessive self-pity*. Everyone pities themselves sometimes. When things do not go just right, it is difficult not to do so. But constant self-pity is highly maladaptive. When one of our graduate students entered our program, he had certain clear disadvantages in terms of preparation, and obviously felt sorry for himself. At that point, others felt sorry for him, too. But after a while, people became annoyed and even angry at his continual self-pity. After a point, everyone expected him to pull himself up by his bootstraps and make a go of things. But the self-pity never seemed to end. A vicious circle ensued in which as he became sorrier and sorrier for himself, others became less and less sorry, until finally they wanted to have little to do with him. He seemed to spend more time feeling sorry for himself than making the effort that would be required so that he no longer would have any cause to feel sorry. Self-pity is not only useless for getting work done, but after a certain point, it tends to put off those who might otherwise be most helpful.

13. *Excessive dependency*. In most of the tasks people face, they are expected to acquire a certain degree of independence. Even in the early elementary grades, children usually are expected gradually to assume some independence—for example, remembering to bring papers home, being able to work independently in the classroom, completing homework on time, and so on. The inability to be independent in age-appropriate ways can seriously compromise children's chances of school success.

Often, people's home lives may ill prepare them for the independence that will later be expected of them. To some extent in school, and especially once they enter a career, they are expected to fend for themselves, and to rely upon others only to the minimally necessary degree. Many students seem not to learn this, and expect others either to do things for them or constantly to show them how to get things done. Without such aid, they are at a total loss. The result is that they often have to seek less responsible jobs, or never do as well as they otherwise might in the job that they have.

In school, as well as in work, do not expect either your

professors or your fellow students to get things done for you. If you want to get them done, the best way to do so is either to do them yourself or to take responsibility for having someone else get them done. Do not expect others to take the responsibility that you yourself must take.

14. *Wallowing in personal difficulties.* Everyone has personal difficulties, but their extent differs widely from one person to another. Some people have repeated tragedies in their lives, whereas others seem to lead charmed existences and almost never encounter difficulties. During the course of people's lives, they can expect some real joys, but also some real sorrows. The important thing is to try to keep both the joys and the sorrows in perspective. Some people let their personal difficulties interfere grossly with their work; others seem to be unaffected in their work. Major life crises will almost always have some effect on one's work, whether one likes it or not. The best thing is to accept that this will happen and take it in stride. It is equally important that people not wallow in their personal difficulties and let them drag down their work and themselves with it. Indeed, in times of personal hardship, their work, as well as other people, may provide them with some of the solace they need. It is a mistake to avoid the personal difficulties that they must often face; it is equally a mistake to allow themselves to be consumed by the difficulties.

15. *Distractibility and lack of concentration.* There are any number of very intelligent people who, despite their high intelligence, never seem to be able to concentrate on anything for very long. They are highly distractible, and tend to have short attention spans. As a result, they tend not to get much done. To some extent, distractibility is an attentional variable over which one does not have total control. If people tend not to be distractible and to have good concentration, then it is not something they have to worry about particularly. If they tend to be distractible, however, and to have difficulty concentrating, then they should do their best to arrange their working environment so as to minimize distractions. In effect, they have to create an environment in which they can achieve their goals. If they do not, they will have difficulty in reaching their goals. Teachers can help children who are unusually distractible by pro-

viding them with an appropriate environment to work in, and by encouraging children to create such an environment for themselves (e.g., by finding a quiet place in which to do homework).

16. *Spreading oneself too thin or too thick.* People with the tendency to spread themselves too thin need to recognize this tendency within themselves and to counteract it as necessary. People who spread themselves too thin sometimes find that they can get nothing done not because they don't work hard enough, but because they are making only little degrees of progress on each of the large number of projects they are pursuing. If they undertake multiple projects, it is important to stagger or otherwise arrange their projects so that they have a reasonable probability of finishing each of them in an acceptable amount of time.

Other people find themselves unable to undertake more than one or at most two things at a given time. This disposition is fine, so long as they can progress through the things they undertake with reasonable dispatch, and not miss opportunities that may present themselves. But undertaking too little at one time can result in missed opportunities and reduced levels of accomplishment. The important thing is to find the right distribution of activities for themselves, and then to maximize their performance within that distribution. They need to avoid undertaking either more or less than they can handle at a single time.

17. *Inability to delay gratification.* Mentioned earlier are the people who always seem to be doing little things at the expense of big things. Some of these are people who simply procrastinate on big things, but others are people who are unable to delay gratification. They reward themselves and others reward them for finishing the little things, but they pass up the larger rewards that they could receive from doing bigger things. Any number of scientists and other scholars fail to undertake the really big projects that could make the critical difference in their careers or repeatedly write short articles instead of books because of their inability to delay the gratification that would come from the completion of a longer but more substantial project. Serious intellectual work occasionally requires one to delay gratification, sometimes for relatively long periods of time.

Without the ability to achieve this delay, they may find themselves passing up the larger rewards that might otherwise await them at the end of the bigger projects.

18. *Inability or unwillingness to see the forest for the trees.* We have worked with several students who have been intellectually very capable but who have been relatively unsuccessful in their careers as students because of their inability to see the forest for the trees: They obsess over small details, and are unwilling or unable to see or deal with the larger picture in the projects they undertake. They become so absorbed with the microstructure of whatever they undertake that they ignore or pay only the most minimal attention to the macrostructure. Similarly, some teachers become so bogged down in the everyday demands of planning individual lessons, correcting papers, and so on, that they lose sight of the broader goals they want to accomplish.

There are times and places where minutiae can become important. In designing computers or spacecraft or cars, for example, even the most minor slips can become major when the product malfunctions. But in many aspects of life, it is necessary to concentrate on the big picture, or at least never to lose sight of it. It is very easy for students to become so bogged down in the day-to-day details of student life that they lose sight of the big picture. If this is happening to them, they need deliberately to set aside time for thinking about large issues. They need to decide that during those times they will think about the meaning of what they are doing and where they wish it to lead them. Without such time, they may find themselves not only losing track of what their goals originally were but losing track as well of how what they are doing will help them reach those goals.

19. *Lack of balance among critical–analytic thinking, creative–synthetic thinking, and practical–contextualized thinking.* There are times in life when one needs to be critical and analytic; there are other times when one should be creative and synthetic; and there are still other times when one needs to apply thinking in practice. It is important to know which times are which. Some students seem frequently to make the wrong judgments on this matter. They complain bitterly that their teachers fail to recognize their creativity

on objective, multiple-choice tests, or they complain that their teachers do not give them credit for how well-organized, if uninspired, their papers are. Although these students may have good analytic and synthetic abilities, they do not know when to apply which ones. It is important to learn what kind of thinking is expected of a person in different kinds of situations, and then to try to do the kind of thinking that is appropriate for the given situations. For example, standardized multiple-choice mental ability tests do not usually provide good opportunities in which to demonstrate creativity, unless they are explicitly designed to measure creativity. Research projects, on the other hand, are excellent opportunities to show creativity. The point is that it is important not only to have analytic, synthetic, and practical abilities, but to know when to use them. Ideally, we want to teach our students to balance the kinds of thinking illustrated by Alice, Barbara, and Celia in Goal 1.

20. *Too little or too much self-confidence.* Everyone needs a hefty measure of self-confidence to get through life. There can be so many blows to one's self-esteem and view of oneself that without self-confidence, we are at the mercy of all the minor and major setbacks that continually confront us. Lack of self-confidence seems to gnaw away at some people's ability to get things done well because they actually seem to realize in their work their own self-doubt: These self-doubts become self-fulfilling prophesies. Self-confidence is often essential for success. After all, if people do not have confidence in themselves, how can they expect others to?

At the same time, it is important not to have too much or misplaced self-confidence. As many students fail through too much self-confidence as through too little. Individuals with too much self-confidence do not know when to admit they are wrong or in need of self-improvement. As a result, they rarely improve as rapidly as they could.

Too little or too much self-confidence can be especially damaging in job interviews. Applicants with too little self-confidence fail to inspire the confidence of those who might employ them. Their lack of self-confidence transfers to the potential employer, who also ends up not having confidence in them. Too much self-confidence can put people off, and lead to resentment and the desire to strike back—to tell the individual in some way that he or she is not as great as he or she thinks. Unfortunately, this striking back can occur in the form of a decision not to hire that person.

Another example is student teaching. Student teachers with excessively low self-confidence tend to have trouble commanding respect from the children in the class. On the other hand, those who are *too* confident may turn off the cooperating teacher or may not recognize that they still have much to learn. It is important, here as elsewhere, to strike just the right balance between too little or too much of a good thing.

## SUMMARY

We have described 20 potential stumbling blocks to the realization of intellectual potential. The material here may seem only vaguely related to the topic of the book—teaching for thinking—or may even seem moralistic. But we have concluded that it is easy, indeed, for those who wish to understand and develop the intellect to become "buried in thought." One must never lose sight of the fact that what really matters in the world is not the level of one's intelligence, but what one achieves with this intelligence. The ultimate goal in understanding and increasing one's intelligence should be the full realization in one's life of the intellectual potential we each have within us.

**1** What are some of the examples of noncognitive variables that may undermine achievement even in highly intelligent individuals?

**2** Which of the problems discussed in this section have you observed in your students? If you could eliminate just one of these problems, which one would you pick and why?

**3** Of the problems discussed in this section, which ones do you think most often affect teachers? In other words, why do intelligent people sometimes fail as teachers?

**1** Answers may include, among other things, lack of motivation; lack of perseverance or the presence of perseveration; fear of failure; using the wrong abilities; constantly letting personal problems get in the way of achievement; misattribution of blame; and excessive dependency.

**2** Answers will vary, but some examples of problems that teachers may find to be especially common or troublesome in children include fear of failure, excessive dependency, lack of impulse control, distractibility, and lack of perseverance.

**3** Answers will vary.

## Goal 7: Teaching Activities: Why Good Thinkers Succeed

Read a biography of a famous individual whom you admire—for example, a well-known scientist, artist, musician, athlete, or political figure. Obviously, famous and successful people usually have talent: successful musicians have musical talent, successful athletes have superior athletic abilities, and so on. However, think about *other* personal qualities that either helped this individual succeed in life (e.g., perseverance in the face of adversity, motivation, a willingness to risk failure) or that hindered him or her (e.g., lack of confidence, being overwhelmed by family problems). Discuss these other personal qualities at length, making specific references to the biography that you chose. Which of these personal qualities do you think were most important in helping this individual to realize his or her achievement, and why?

## GOAL 7: SUGGESTED READINGS

Ceci, S. J., & Liker, J. (1986). Academic and nonacademic intelligence: An experimental separation. In R. J. Sternberg & R. K. Wagner (Eds.), *Practical intelligence: Nature and origins of competence in the everyday world* (pp. 119–142). New York: Cambridge University Press.

Cole, M., Gay, J., Glick, J., & Sharp, D. W. (1971). *The cultural context of learning and thinking*. New York: Basic Books.

Sternberg, R. J. (1986). *Intelligence applied: Understanding and increasing your intellectual skills*. San Diego: Harcourt Brace Jovanovich.

# final review and summary

We have attempted in this book to present a theoretical framework for understanding, teaching, and assessing intelligent thinking in the context of the classroom and of life in general. We have also tried to show teachers how they can use this framework to enhance their instruction and assessment. Ultimately, we believe that there are three keys students need in order to unchain the thinking abilities they already have within them.

The first is instruction and assessment that teach for thinking. In this book, you have learned a variety of strategies you can use to teach any subject matter in a way that gives students this key. Students not only learn to think better when they are taught in a thinking-based way; they also remember material better, simply because they have to think about the material while they learn it. By thinking to learn, students learn to think.

The second key is practice and then more practice with the three ways of thinking: Students need to become involved actively as well as passively in the three ways of thinking. A teacher can teach in all three ways, but the students will not learn if they are not given chances to apply the three ways in their own problem formulation and problem solving.

The third and perhaps most important key is being a role model. As a teacher, you need to be a role model for how to think. If you tell students to think in one way but teach in another, or even if you teach lessons in one way, but then act with students at other times in another way, students are more likely to do as you do than to do as you say. What we often remember best about our teachers is not exactly what they taught, but what they were like. We all need to act in ways that will lead students to remember us as actively doing ourselves what we always told them they should do themselves.

What are the main points to apply in your teaching for thinking? We believe they are these:

1. Good thinking has analytical, creative, and practical aspects. Underlying these aspects of thinking are at least seven fundamental skills: (a) problem identification, (b) process selection, (c) representation of information, (d) strategy formation, (e) allocation of resources, (f) solution monitoring, and (g) evaluating solutions.

2. Three strategies for teaching in classrooms are (a) didactic, (b) fact-based questioning, and (c) thinking-based questioning (a dialogical approach). The thinking-based, dialogical approach best teaches children how to think ef-

fectively, but a combination of the three approaches is ideal for helping children learn and think well.

3. Learning how to ask questions plays as important a role in the development of thinking as does learning how to answer questions. Teachers can help children develop questioning strategies by encouraging the children to consider alternative explanation of phenomena as well as to consider means of evaluating these explanations.

4. In teaching children to develop their analytical abilities, you want to give children opportunities to compare, contrast, analyze, evaluate, and explain. In helping children develop creative abilities, you want to give the children opportunities to create, invent, imagine, and suppose. In teaching them to develop their practical abilities, you want to give the children opportunities to use, utilize, apply, and implement. These skills can be taught in a four-step instructional model: (a) familiarization, (b) intragroup problem solving, (c) intergroup problem solving, and (d) individual problem solving.

5. Insightful problem solving is particularly important in life, but is typically underemphasized in schools. Insight can involve three distinct processes of (a) selective encoding, (b) selective combination, and (c) selective comparison.

6. Good teaching for thinking requires understanding of some of the major principles and pitfalls of such teaching. Examples of some principles are the need to emphasize problem recognition and definition as well as solution, and the need to present children with a balance of well-structured and ill-structured problems. Examples of pitfalls are the false beliefs that teachers are not also learners, and that the correct answer is more important than the process used to arrive at that answer.

7. Good thinkers often do not succeed as well as they could because of emotional and motivational blocks, such as lack

of impulse control, lack of perseverance, and inability to translate thought into action.

By following the principles and applying the techniques described in this book, teachers can immediately and substantively improve the effectiveness of their teaching for thinking.

# glossary

**ability**— a developed skill for performing a certain class of tasks.

**analytical thinking**— thinking that dissects, critiques, evaluates, and judges.

**creative thinking**— thinking that is novel, task-appropriate, and of high quality.

**critical thinking**— narrowly, analytical thinking; broadly, any higher order thinking.

**dialogical approach**— an approach to teaching that encourages questioning and consideration of alternative points of view.

**didactic approach**— a distinctively fact-oriented approach to teaching whereby the teacher presents material through direct instruction.

**fact-based questioning**— an approach to teaching whereby teachers ask children fact-based questions as an integral part of a lesson.

**ill-structured problem**— a problem with no preset, well-defined path or solution.

**insight**— a restructuring of a problem in a way that facilitates solutions, or the appearance of a nonobvious solution to a problem.

**intelligence**— the ability purposively to adapt to, select, and shape environment.

**intergroup problem solving**— discussing solutions to a problem across groups.

**internalization**— incorporating into oneself thoughts and behavior patterns one observes in the social environment.

**intragroup problem solving**— formulating and discussing solutions to a problem within a given group.

**mainstreaming**— placing exceptional children in a regular classroom.

**mastery learning**— learning to a high, preset level of understanding.

**mediated learning experience**— explanation and interpretation of the environment for a learner in order to facilitate learning.

**practical thinking**— thinking with application to a person's own life.

**problem**— an obstacle to the fulfillment of a goal.

**selective combination**— putting together in nonobvious ways pieces of information needed to solve a problem.

**selective comparison**— drawing on past information to solve a problem in the present where the relevance of the past information is not immediately obvious.

**selective encoding**— sifting out relevant from irrelevant information in problem solving where it is not obvious which information is relevant.

**strategy**— an ordered set of processes for accomplishing a goal.

**triarchic theory**— a theory of intelligence according to which intelligence comprises analytical, creative, and practical aspects.

**well-structured problem**— a problem with a preset, well-defined path to the solution.

# references

Albert, R. S. (1983). *Genius and eminence*. New York: Pergamon Press.

Arlin, P. K. (1990). Wisdom: The art of problem finding. In R. J. Sternberg (Ed.), *Wisdom: Its nature, origins, and development* (pp. 230–243). New York: Cambridge University Press.

Baron, J. B., & Sternberg, R. J. (Eds.). (1987). *Teaching thinking skills: Theory and practice*. New York: Freeman.

Bransford, J., & Stein, B. (1993). *The ideal problem solver* (2nd ed.). San Francisco: Freeman.

Butterfield, E. C., & Belmont, J. M. (1977). Assessing and improving the cognition of mentally retarded people. In I. Bialer & M. Sternlicht (Eds.), *Psychology of mental retarda-*

*tion: Issues and approaches.* New York: Psychological Dimensions.

Campione, J. C., & Brown, A. L. (1979). Toward a theory of intelligence: Contributions from research with retarded children. In R. J. Sternberg & D. K. Detterman (Eds.), *Human Intelligence: Perspectives on its theory and measurement* (pp. 139–164). Norwood, NJ: Ablex.

Carroll, J. B. (1981). Ability and task difficulty in cognitive psychology. *Educational Researcher, 10,* 11–21.

Ceci, S. J., & Liker, J. (1986). Academic and nonacademic intelligence: An experimental separation. In R. J. Sternberg & Rick Wagner (Eds.), *Practical intelligence: Nature and origins of competence in the everyday world* (pp. 119–142). New York: Cambridge University Press.

Chipman, S., Siegel, J., & Glaser, R. (Eds.). (1985). *Thinking and learning skills: Current research and open questions* (Vol. 2). Hillsdale, NJ: Erlbaum.

Cole, M., Gay, J., Glick, J., & Sharp, D. W. (1971). *The cultural context of learning and thinking.* New York: Basic Books.

Covington, M. V., Crutchfield, R. S., Davies, L., & Olton, R. M. (1974). *The productive thinking program: A course in learning to think.* Columbus, OH: Charles E. Merrill.

Davidson, J. E., & Sternberg, R. J. (1984). The role of insight in intellectual giftedness. *Gifted Child Quarterly, 28,* 58–64.

Feuerstein, R. (1979). *The dynamic assessment of retarded performers: The learning potential assessment device, theory, instruments, and techniques.* Baltimore, MD: University Park Press.

Feuerstein, R. (1980). *Instrumental enrichment: An intervention program for cognitive modifiability.* Baltimore, MD: University Park Press.